BEING LAKOTA

BEING LAKOTA

Identity and Tradition on Pine Ridge Reservation

Larissa Petrillo in collaboration
with Melda and Lupe Trejo

University of Nebraska Press • Lincoln & London

Library of Congress Cataloging-
in-Publication Data
Petrillo, Larissa.
Being Lakota : identity and tradition on
Pine Ridge Reservation / Larissa Petrillo
in collaboration with Melda and Lupe Trejo.
p. cm.
Includes bibliographical references and index.
ISBN-13: 978-0-8032-3750-6 (cloth : alk. paper)
ISBN-10: 0-8032-3750-2 (cloth : alk. paper)
1. Dakota Indians—South Dakota—Pine Ridge
Indian Reservation—Ethnic identity. 2. Dakota
Indians—South Dakota—Pine Ridge Indian
Reservation—History. 3. Dakota Indians—
South Dakota—Pine Ridge Indian Reservation
—Social life and customs. 4. Pine Ridge Indian
Reservation (S.D.)—History. 5. Pine Ridge
Indian Reservation (S.D.)—Social life and customs.
I. Trejo, Melda, 1939– II. Trejo, Lupe, 1938–1999.
III. Title.
E99.D1P48 2007
305.897'5244078366—dc22
2006021199

Dedicated to
"Down East"

CONTENTS

ACKNOWLEDGMENTS

I would not have been able to write this book without Melda and Lupe Trejo and the welcoming and thoughtful people in the Lakota community. Driving up and over the driveway that leads to the log home "down east" is always like coming home in a way. Melda and Lupe are both such special people, and I have been truly changed by our time together. I'm the same age as the younger of Melda and Lupe's children, and they have all been great friends to me. I've appreciated their genuine warmth and straightforward support. Thanks to Barbara, Debbie, Jimmy, Lucy, Marcus, Robert, Ruben, and Raymond. And thanks to all of the grandchildren for always keeping me on my toes, and for their affection and spirit.

I recall an enjoyable road trip to Scottsbluff, Nebraska, with Melda and her cousin Edna Janis. We met with Melda's brother Norman and his wife and Lupe's sister Cleo. Lupe's other sister, Susie Dominguez, shared some wonderful photographs. I was pleased to meet Joe Trejo and other members of Lupe's family as well.

There have been so many friends at the Sun Dances over the years, both from the community and from further afield. Sometimes, people I've come to know very well over the years; sometimes those whom I might just know through a common and reassuring nod. Additionally, Lorena Cobb of Merriman, Nebraska, took good care of me. Her strength, as a mature woman who runs a ranch on her own, is worthy of a book in itself.

To my proofreaders, Brenda Trejo and Kay Koppedrayer, who didn't really have to help me but did anyhow: you have both been so encouraging and provided wonderful comments during the many stages of this work. Unfailing, caring, and kindhearted.

Again, thanks to Kay and her husband, Jaap, for first taking me to Pine Ridge Reservation and introducing me to Melda and Lupe. That was a great road trip that started off what has been a life's journey. Kay has been a great friend, and we've had many good conversations traveling across the prairies.

Thanks to Ray Bucko, who read the manuscript in several different versions and was a true inspiration with his own work in the Lakota community. His sense of humor and his remarkable energy are, no doubt, encouraging to everyone around him.

In the academic community, many people at the University of British Columbia (UBC) have been helpful. Margery Fee's patience, enthusiasm, and support when others may have tired at what was a long writing process meant that this work became what I always knew it could be. Jo Fiske, Jo-Ann Archibald, and Nikki Strong-Boag were also careful and encouraging readers. Thanks as well to other readers at UBC: Laurie Ricou, Susanna Egan, and Jean Barman.

The University of Nebraska Press found great reviewers for this manuscript; they contributed substantially to the final product. I have felt lucky to have such valuable feedback at several points in the publication process.

Of my family members, my mother, brother, and husband have all traveled to Pine Ridge Reservation with me. My mother, also a great proofreader, is still the source of stories on the reservation after a fall in the creek "down east." My brother took an interest in things that were important to me, and he was a truly fun travel partner. Jason, my husband, helped me first put this all to paper sitting around a campfire years ago and has, since then, made it all real. My father has always had faith in my ideas, and his trust and support meant I could do all of the things that mattered to me. Thanks to all of my friends and family. And to my very own grandparents, because this work has inspired us to go ahead and record our own family history.

Thank you, again, to my coauthors, Melda and Lupe Trejo. Also, to others who have done similar work and continue to work toward helping us all understand one another.

Melda and Lupe Trejo on "Being Indian"

Being Lakota: Identity and Tradition on Pine Ridge Reservation explores contemporary Lakota identity and tradition, as informed by the life story narratives of Melda and Lupe Trejo. Melda Red Bear (Lakota) was born in 1939 on Pine Ridge (Oglala Lakota/Sioux) Reservation in South Dakota. Her husband, Lupe Trejo (1938–99), is Mexican and has been a long-term resident of the reservation. In their forty years together, Melda and Lupe raised eleven children and supported themselves as migrant workers. Since 1988 they have held a Sun Dance ceremony on the Red Bear land on Pine Ridge Reservation. In their life stories, Melda and Lupe emphasize the importance of the Sun Dance ceremony and convey their understanding of Lakota tradition to their relations. They define themselves through their spiritual practice in the Sun Dance, and they situate themselves and their Sun Dance amid the controversies that surround authentic practices and the participation of outsiders in the ceremony. Because of Lupe's Mexican heritage, Melda and Lupe negotiate their ties to Lakota culture in different ways, and their explication of affiliation and belonging is precisely what makes their life stories so relevant to a contemporary understanding of Lakota identity.

In this book I provide an interpretive framework, supported by life stories as well as critical and ethnographic material, for the analysis of Melda and Lupe's account. I also provide the context and method that informed my understanding, as a non-Native scholar, of the life story narratives of this Lakota/Mexican couple. My focus is ethnic identity, and this interest has been prompted by feminist questions about how to act politically without using normalizing categories, such as "woman." I find being "Indian" especially interesting given the ways such an identity is rooted in ideas of the past but negotiated in the present.[1] That said, my ideas about feminism, ethnicity, and collaborative work changed over the course of this project—revisions that this text recounts. Life story narratives provide critical insight into how individuals derive agency. As "the power to choose, to act, to change oneself and/or the world" (Edelstein 102), *agency* means that individuals can make claims to legitimacy while also acknowledging that identities are multiple and constructed. Consequently, my task is not to define the "real Indian" but to examine the ways that Melda and Lupe talk about *being* Indian.[2]

The Sun Dance is emblematic of ongoing retraditionalization efforts in many Native communities. It was reintroduced in the 1970s and 1980s and is now prevalent on both Pine Ridge Reservation and the neighboring reservation, Rosebud.[3] The number of ceremonies has been increasing exponentially since that time, and there are presently many concurrent Sun Dances throughout the summer period. The ceremony was effectively curtailed by the Bureau of Indian Affairs (BIA) in the late nineteenth century.[4] Following revitalization efforts, the Crow Dog Sun Dance, in 1973, was the first widely accessible autonomous ceremony. It was held on Rosebud Reservation by Henry Crow Dog (Lakota) and his son, Leonard Crow Dog, a medicine man who is often associated with the American Indian Movement (AIM).[5] The Red Power movement of the 1970s was characterized by spiritual revitalization, political protest, and demands for treaty rights.[6] The activist movement grew out of the civil rights era of the 1960s and came to be associated with the reintroduction of spiritual practices.[7] Melda says, "I don't know what year, but Sun Dancing didn't really start until AIM people. In 1973. Wounded Knee and after that. Sun Dances started." She is referring to the 1973 occupation of the site of the Wounded Knee massacre by Lakota traditionalists and members of AIM in an effort to draw attention to federal, tribal, and local grievances.[8] Melda and Lupe do not explicitly refer to the political activity on the reservation at that time. They associate the period only with its spiritual resurgence, and they align themselves with this resurgence.

Melda positions herself as a Lakota woman by claiming a set of
experiences that are lineal, cultural, and political, while Lupe necessarily negotiates a different set of experiences in his life as a Mexican
American. Melda's great-great-grandfather was an Indian scout for
the U.S. Army and the third cousin of the well-known Lakota warrior
Crazy Horse (Kadlecek and Kadlecek 139, 161). Howard Red Bear, her
paternal great-uncle, was an Indian scout for the U.S. Army. He served
under Company I, 2nd regiment, and was stationed at Fort Crook.
Philip Runs Along the Edge Red Bear, Melda's great-grandfather, born
in the mid-1800s, was influential in bringing peyote to South Dakota
in 1914 and in establishing the Native American Church. The Native
American Church is a pan-Indian Christian religion that involves the
use of peyote and, in Red Bear's case, the traditional pipe. Melda attended Native American Church meetings that were run by her father until she was sixteen years old. She grew up speaking the Lakota
language, and she continues to speak Lakota with those who know
the language. Lupe can understand much of the Lakota language, but
he speaks only English and Spanish. His father came to the United
States from Mexico without any papers when he was a young boy.
His mother was born in Texas and primarily spoke Spanish. Lupe was
born in Coleman, Texas, and in his youth he spent seven years training
for the priesthood at a seminary. Lupe is proud of what he describes
as his Aztec heritage, and he visited his aunts and uncles in Mexico at
one point with his father. He worked on farms for much of his life and
worked for one man on the same farm in Nebraska for almost forty
years. Lupe identifies as an Aztec Indian, emphasizes his Mexican and
Indian cultural ties, and maintains these connections despite being
grounded in the Lakota cultural tradition on Pine Ridge Reservation.

I was introduced to Melda and Lupe through a mutual friend in
1995, and I developed an enduring friendship with them prior to our
decision to collaborate in recording their storytelling sessions (1997–
98). Ten ninety-minute tapes were recorded, and conversations—both
social and for the purposes of this book—have continued since that

time. I have been going to the reservation for ten years now, for weeks or months at a time. In our sessions, the process of recording was largely undirected. I avoided asking leading questions and allowed for an open-ended session. Over the course of our developing friendship, I had already heard Melda tell repeatedly the stories that she values to numerous different people on the reservation. I only needed to prompt her recall of those stories. Melda served a similar function in eliciting stories from Lupe that she had already heard. This written account has, at times, been edited from more open-ended discussions among Melda, Lupe, and myself so as to now read as uninterrupted narratives; at other times the conversational exchanges are left intact. The resulting work is based, in part, on feedback from the academic and reservation communities connected to the project. Members of the Trejo family have been involved in each step of the writing process, and our relationship continues outside the research context.

Overview and Outline of Chapters

In this book, the chapters alternate between those that convey Melda and Lupe Trejo's life story narratives and those that further explore the material produced by our collaboration. In transcribing their spoken words onto these pages, I have retained the original language used by Melda and Lupe in an effort to convey the particular qualities of their speech.

The chapters correspond with one another, in each case initiated with a narrative from Melda and Lupe and a chapter that follows to put forward my own material. There are three broad sections: family, identity, and tradition. The first section introduces Melda and Lupe and identifies my role in the project. Chapter 1 provides an overview of the reservation and of my experiences in the community as well as commentary on Lakota tradition. In chapter 2 Melda and Lupe provide an account of key moments in their lives. Melda describes her family's move from the reservation in the 1950s and her subsequent return to the Red Bear land in South Dakota. Lupe similarly recounts his life experiences, emphasizing his personal vision of an eagle and his subsequent decision to move toward Lakota tradition. In this instance only, Melda and Lupe's narrative chapter is followed by another life story account. In chapter 3 Melda describes her childhood as well as how she came to meet and marry Lupe. Their union was celebrated in 1998 with the renewal of their wedding vows for their fortieth anniversary. Chapter 4 is the first account I provide about our collaboration. I discuss questions associated with knowledge and power and trace how my ideas about the project changed over time. In chapter 5 Lupe describes his childhood, and he and Melda discuss their lives as young parents and their experiences as migrant workers. Lupe's ethnicity is the focus of the discussion in chapter 6.

The second section of the book deals more seriously with identity. In chapter 7, Melda and Lupe tell how they came to hold a Sun Dance. The timeline of their move toward the Sun Dance is sometimes difficult to determine. This is because they are not speaking about time as a linear marker; rather, they are describing life passages and ceremonial cycles. The unexpected and exceptional events that take place over a forty-year period are retold in this chapter with wonder and sincerity. Chapter 8 discusses the retraditionalization characteristic of the period following the passage of the American Indian Religious Freedom Act (1978). Ceremonies that had been practiced underground became more widely accessible at that time. In this case I focus on Melda's life and how she supports the generational ties of the Lakota community. In chapter 9, Melda and Lupe talk about the ways they have upheld both Lakota tradition and Lupe's Mexican heritage. They also describe intermarriage and the bicultural associations of their family. Racial issues are correspondingly analyzed in chapter 10.

The third section of the book examines Lakota beliefs and practices in greater depth. In chapter 11, Melda and Lupe discuss the changes in tradition that have occurred both historically and in the contemporary era. They talk about the Ghost Dance, Christianity, and the Native American Church. I examine the policing of tradition that has resulted from the proliferation of such spiritual practices in chapter 12. In this chapter I also discuss prayer, ceremony, and Lakota religious beliefs to preface Melda and Lupe's discussions of these subjects in the final narrative chapter. In chapter 13, Melda and Lupe talk about spiritual authority as a regenerative practice. They describe how they have constantly negotiated and learned about what they term "traditional ways" and how they pass these ideals on to others. I investigate the difference between Lakota spiritual practices and academic ethics protocols in chapter 14. This chapter also includes a sustained narrative by Melda about her grandson taking part in the Sun Dance, and I recount the different ways that I have understood this story over time. The conclusion describes how meanings can vary with the adoption of different viewpoints and how the project itself constantly involved bringing different standpoints into relation with one another.

Melda and Lupe's life story narratives reveal that contemporary Lakota identity includes colonial discourses, strategic responses to such impositions, *and* an autonomous indigenous system of beliefs. Melda and Lupe speak about a way of knowing the world that is firmly rooted in Lakota cosmology, spiritual principles, and traditional practices. Their epistemological framework involves the Lakota spiritual belief that we are all related, embodied in the prayer *Mitakuye 'oyasin* ("All My Relations"). From a colonial perspective, Indian identity compels definition. Consequently, Melda and Lupe differentiate between "Indian" and "white" in ways that contest relatedness. Traditionally, however, constructing and negotiating identity and tradition through prayer, ceremony, and storytelling functions to maintain all that is related. I had accordingly anticipated Melda and Lupe's engagement with "Indian pride," but I had not realized the degree to which personal and spiritual elements might combine at present in everyday life. Witnessing these convergences prompted me to recognize that Lakota beliefs form an epistemological tradition, a way of thinking.

PART I

Family

Impressions

The Lakotas (Teton), also called the Oglala Sioux, are part of a larger group that includes the Dakotas (Santee), Nakotas (Yankton), and other Lakota bands, collectively known as the Sioux Indians.[1] The Lakotas have been referred to as "the archetypal Indian in the American imagination" and have been popularized in many of the Indian stereotypes associated with the "Wild West" (Bucko 34). Pine Ridge Reservation, located in the plains of southwestern South Dakota, is the second-largest reservation in the United States, with an estimated trust acreage of 1,783,741 square miles (Federal Emergency Management Agency [FEMA]). Its American Indian population is estimated to be between 14,295 (U.S. Census Bureau, 2000) and 39,734 (FEMA).

The territory of the Great Sioux Reservation was established with the revision of the Fort Laramie Treaty in 1868. The Lakota people began living inside the boundaries of the reservation primarily in the 1880s, although the order for Indians to return to tribal lands was issued in 1876. In 1887 the General Allotment Act (also known as the Dawes Act) legislated that land be divided into private allotments to be held in trust for twenty-five years. The reservation is divided into nine districts, based on historical cattle issue stations. The Red Bear land, located in Bennett County, lies in the area of Pass Creek, which comprises Allen Village (the closest housing district), Bear Creek, Yellow Bear, North, and Corn Creek.[2] The area east of Allen is currently outside the reservation boundary, subsequent to the leasing of neighboring parcels of land, but the only access road is via the reservation and it is widely perceived as reservation land.

Melda lives on the Red Bear land, near Allen in Bennett County; the Trejo family refers to this area as "down east." It is characteristic of much of the rural parts of the reservation. The log house on the Red Bear land lies beside a slow-moving creek and is set in a valley

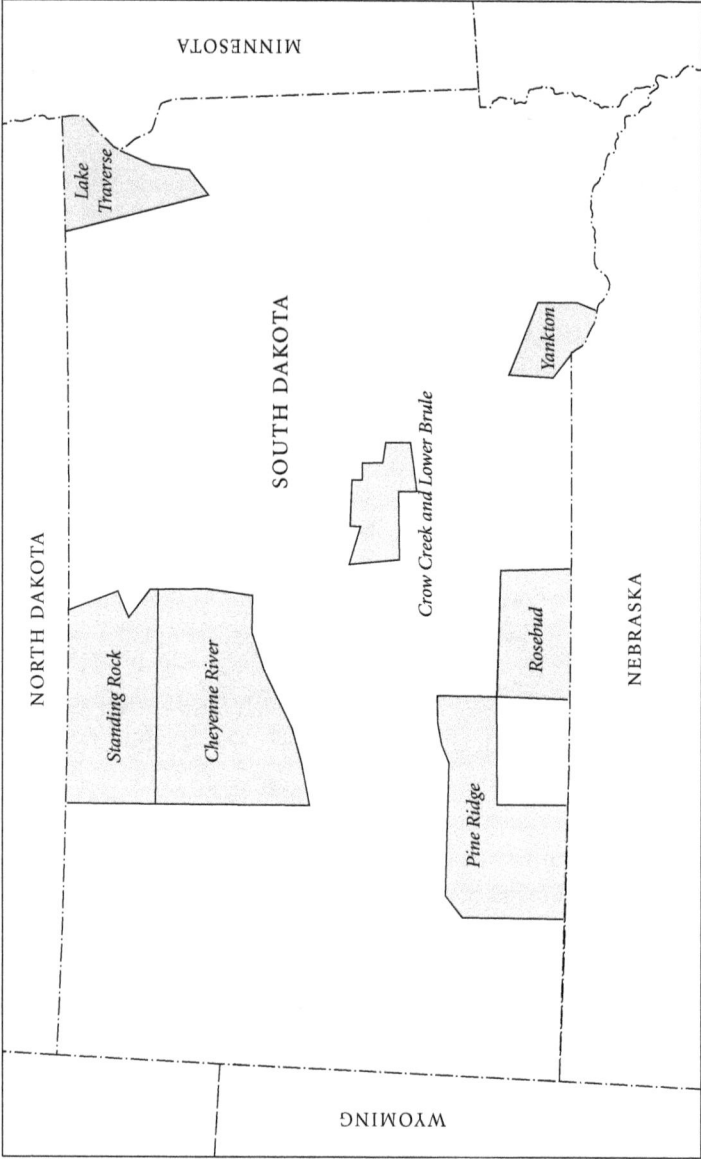

Map 1. Reservations in South Dakota

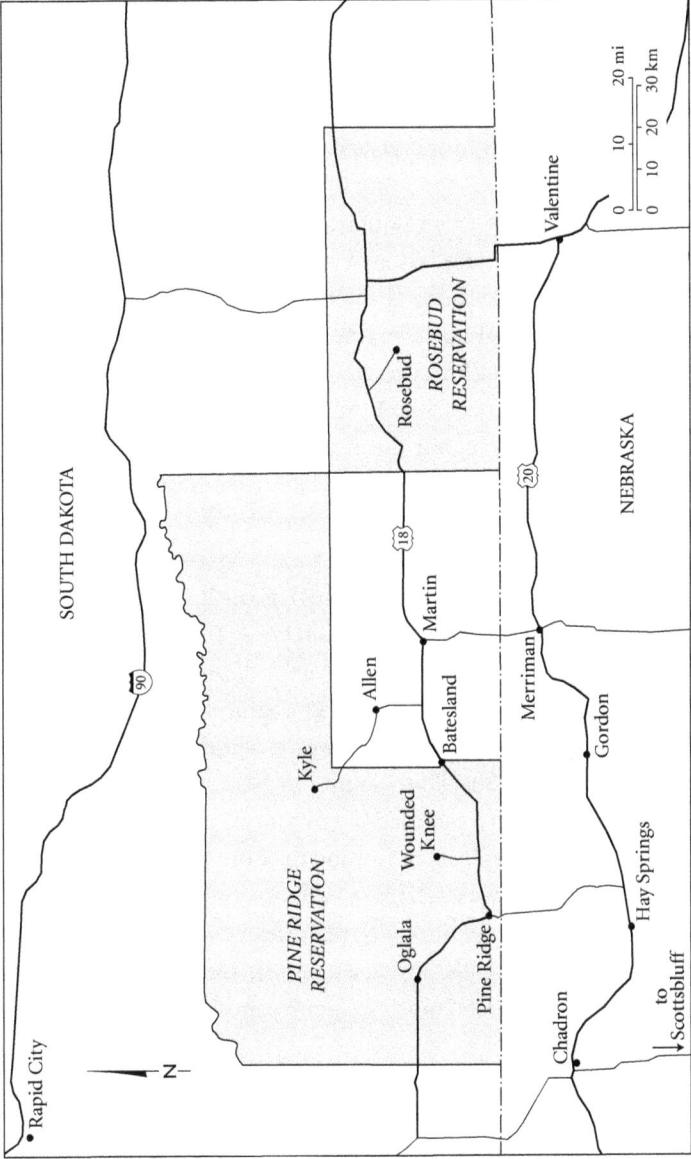

Map 2. Pine Ridge Reservation and surrounding area

surrounded by pine-forested hills. A freshwater spring on the land bubbles up from the ground, and many tobacco offerings have been placed at this spot. During the frequent South Dakota thunderstorms, the lightning touches down along the surrounding ridges; the valley lies protected below. The driveway that leads into the property runs up and over these hills and is often washed out with the rain, but it dries quickly in the hot summers. Sage, echinacea, *tipsila* (wild turnip), and wildflowers grow in the surrounding grasslands. In the wintertime, the log home is heated with an old woodstove and family and visitors gather in the large main room, which is decorated with many family photographs. During the summer, much of the time is spent near a tarpaulin-covered cookshack on old chairs that are scattered around the outside of the house.

Highway 18 runs along the state line connecting Pine Ridge Reservation to Martin, its closest sizable off-reservation neighbor. Martin is a ranching town with a prominent history as the seat of Bennett County. Its population of 1,106 is virtually split between Indians and non-Indians (2000 census). Paula L. Wagoner describes both the tensions and the affiliations between the two areas in *"They Treated Us Just Like Indians": The Worlds of Bennett County, South Dakota* (2002). Owing to the high price of groceries in Martin, Melda often drives an extra twenty minutes to Gordon to do her shopping. Gordon is in Sheridan County in Nebraska. It is similarly a ranching town, with a population of 1,756, although there are fewer Native American residents in Gordon than in Martin (2000 census). For even larger purchases, trips would sometimes be made to Rapid City, South Dakota. Additionally, many friends and family continue to live in Scottsbluff, Nebraska, a city near the North Platte River, with a larger population of 14,732 (2000 census) and a more diverse ethnic population.

I typically drive to South Dakota from Vancouver, Canada, to stay with Melda and Lupe. I have been doing this nearly every summer since 1995, sometimes also visiting in the spring and fall. In 1997 I stayed for a few months, but since then I have usually stayed for a few weeks. During longer visits I have used a trailer that sits behind the log house "down east." I have also stayed with Melda and Lupe in their home in the HUD (Housing and Urban Development) houses in Allen when they were living there for a few years. Sometimes I also found a home in an air-conditioned trailer in Merriman, Nebraska. Here I had developed a friendship with a non-Native rancher, Lorena Cobb, and she provided me with a companion perspective to the history and culture of the plains. More often, though, I simply sleep in my tent in the fields "down east," and at times Sun Dancers and other visitors camp in the fields with me. The drive to South Dakota has become very familiar. I follow the interstate highway I-90 over the Continental Divide, stopping at the same campgrounds and small motels along the way. In Montana I begin to head south and cut through Wyoming on my way to Nebraska and South Dakota. I pass the Little Bighorn battlefield, but I've never stopped there. After the three-day drive, I'm always eager to settle in to take part in the cooking, the visiting, and the general joking around that accompanies my visits.

Humor is an element that often gets omitted in discussions about Native American communities, but to me it is one of the defining qualities of the reservation. Speaking of humor, a woman from AlterNative, a Native Canadian theater troupe, elaborates on this essential aspect of Native communities:

> Humor is transforming. It can take you to another place—good, bad, ugly, things you want to hide or things you want to celebrate—because . . . I come from a tradition where even in ceremony—that is the most crucial, the most serious part of our lives—there is joke telling, there's people playing the trickster, showing their comic wit. And, I think that that is distinctly Native because I would not find that in a Catholic church or a Protestant church, they weren't doing that when I visited the Vatican. You know they weren't cracking jokes and having a good time. So, because our stories are transforming, humor is one of our elemental tools that we've used throughout our experience. And, I don't see us as just being an oppressed people, we're a people that experience things and we talk about them. (*Redskins*)

One of the things I share with both Melda and Lupe is a love of humor. Even when Melda is describing hardships, her tone is often light-hearted and always encouraging; she enjoys telling stories and laughs often during her conversations. Like Melda, I'm known as someone who giggles. I like to crack jokes, and I laugh at anyone who is even remotely funny. This has been, in part, what has made it so easy to share common ground with those on the reservation. I can think of one particular instance when an elaborate tale was concocted that showcased me as the perpetrator on the television show *Cops*. The scenario had several policemen chasing me to the Canadian border. This story developed because we had inadvertently started a grass fire "down east." It was unanimously decided that I should be blamed for the mishap. We had been cleaning up the Red Bear/Native American Church cemetery and decided to set a grass fire to generate new field growth. I was with Melda and other family members when the fire very rapidly grew out of control. We did get the fire to stop, but the stories about *Cops* certainly continued for some time.

The trips to the reservation are also accompanied by incredible loss, particularly in the staggering number of people who have died. They are family members, neighbors, those who have been involved in ceremonies, and those who have supported the traditional community as it has emerged in Melda and Lupe's lives. I will mention only those cited in the life story accounts who have died in the past few years, since our recording was finished. I have had the privilege of meeting each of these individuals and will miss them as well. Uncle Tom, Tom Crow, is referred to as an uncle in Lakota, although he is technically a cousin. He was one of the oldest people in the immediate area of Allen, and he was well known for his spiritual counseling and historical knowledge. His passing in September 2003 was a significant loss to the Lakota community and, more personally, to those who enjoyed his mature and even presence. Melda's brother Solomon Red Bear, or Junior, died in July 2004. He was a minister in the Native American Church and carried on the teachings of his father and great-grandfather. Christine Crow Dog died in the spring of 2005. The daughter of Mary Gertrude and Henry Crow Dog, she had been married to Melda's oldest brother, Albert. Diane Crow Dog also died in early 2006. Melda and Lupe also mention others who have since passed away: Eugene and his son Orville Reddest, who ran a Sun Dance near the Badlands in South Dakota, and Earl Swift Hawk, who, for so many years, ran the Sun Dance that Melda and Lupe held "down east." In terms of those who have died, there have been many other people—whom I have both known and not known—who were often far too young and who brought strength to the community through songs, guidance, or sometimes through their endearing badgering and joking.

The drive to South Dakota in the summer of 1999 was significant because that was the year Lupe died. I was driving down for a regular visit when Lupe died unexpectedly of a heart attack while doing farmwork in Scottsbluff. When I arrived there were many more friends and family gathered "down east" than usual. It was an absolute shock; I discovered that everyone was there for Lupe's funeral. The funeral itself was unique, with observances by Mexican American family members, Lakota spiritual practitioners, and Native American Church ministers. It was an example of everyone praying together that would have made Lupe very happy. Lupe was buried in the cemetery "down east" near Allen. The cemetery can be seen from the gravel road that leads to the log house, and people often look up at the hillside as they drive by. To me, Lupe is alive through his stories and through the memories we all have of him. His life story account is thoughtful; he is looking back on his life with fulfillment. He tends to joke and make light of situations, but underneath this more public image is an inclination toward philosophical reflection. He brought a distinctive contemplation to his life and conveyed to me a singular presence that was both understated and inquiring. Reflecting on his father's teachings, he says, "And, now, to this day, I know what he means." In this way he passes on the understanding that he developed over his full and contented life.

Melda and Lupe articulate identity, in part, by associating their cultural values with prayer and ceremony. *Tunkashila* literally means "grandfather" and is an invocation of the Lakota conception of the godhead. *Wakan Tanka* refers to God or the Great Spirit. It is translated, like *wakan* (sacred power), as meaning something that is powerful, mysterious, unknowable, or holy. For the purposes of this discussion, the details of Lakota ceremonies matter much less than the ways that Melda and Lupe discuss their relationships to these ceremonies.[3] There are many different sacred rites in Lakota tradition, including the sweat lodge (*inipi*) or purification rite; the funeral practices, or "keeping of the soul"; the vision quest, or "crying for a vision" (*hambleceya*); the Sun Dance (*Wi wanyang wacipi*); the adoption ceremony, or "making of relatives" (*hunka*); and the puberty rites.[4] Additionally, the *yuwipi* and other ceremonies involve spiritual practitioners acting on behalf of the community or individuals in need.[5] The *hambleceya* is often also called "going up the hill," and it is a key factor in ritual legitimation. For the *hambleceya*, individuals are brought to a hilltop by those in the community. They are left alone in prayer at this chosen spot as they seek a vision or spiritual understanding.

In the Lakota community, the pipe continues to be used "to re-member White Buffalo Cow [Calf] Woman and serves as a medium of purification and prayer" (Bucko 55). Prayers are made to the four directions—north, south, east, and west—and each direction is associated with a specific color and set of symbols.[6] For those who are unaware of the ceremony, the Sun Dance should be distinguished from the popularly conceived image of the men's traditional dance of the contemporary powwow. In reference to the powwow, "traditional" entails a particular style of dance, most recognizable because of its use of the men's headdress. The intertribal powwow (*wacipi*), which started in the 1930s, became increasingly popular during the 1950s and 1960s, and Melda and Lupe met at a powwow in 1957.[7] In the Sun Dance, on the other hand, the dancers continually gaze at the sun while dancing and fasting, and they commit to doing this for a period of one to four days. The ceremony provides strength, and each year the dancers individually make a pledge to dance for "the people" or for specific individuals in need.

The Trejos are, as Melda says, also a family that has "two cultures." Melda and Lupe talk about intermarriage and racial issues. They emphasize Lupe's Mexican heritage in describing their visit to Mexico with Lupe's father, and they make cultural observations about this Mexican community as "outsiders." Melda further makes observations about Mexican tradition in describing the *quincinara*, a rite of passage for young girls as they turn fifteen. She also discusses the healing practices, or *curanderismo*, of Lupe's mother. In a more recent conversation, after our recording sessions, Melda conveyed further stories about her paternal great-grandparents, Philip Runs Along the Edge Red Bear and his wife, Luisa Martinez (or Shell Woman). She said that I should include the material, and I suspect that the emphasis on her own Mexican ancestry derives in part from my initial tendency, described in a later chapter, to downplay Lupe's Mexican heritage. She says that Luisa Martinez Runs Along the Edge was from Mexico and is an Aztec. Luisa apparently used the name Shell Woman so that she could avoid using her Mexican name on the reservation. Philip Runs Along the Edge traveled to "Washte country" (Arizona/New Mexico) every winter, and the people there arranged a marriage between him and Luisa. Luisa's father was reputed to be a conquistador, Hernandez Martinez, and Luisa kept his conquistador helmet with her in South Dakota. Melda jokes, "Philip must have been really handsome to get such an important woman." In many ways, these great-grandparents embody the characteristics that Melda and Lupe choose to pass on about their own lives in that their lives involve both intermarriage and the support of traditional practices.

Lakota tradition is constantly negotiated, at the individual and the community level, as something that is both old and new. Drawing on the past, tradition is constituted as something current and venerable in the present. Consequently, Lakota tradition can be conceived in a number of ways. As Melda and Lupe characterize it, that which is "traditional" is necessarily constantly changing. These changes result from the responses to colonial impositions, but they also occur because all cultural traditions must constantly change. Dakota scholar Vine Deloria Jr. summarizes some of these ideas; specifically, he contests the idea that Lakota tradition—and, I would suggest, Indian identity—has ever been associated only with the past: "We must be confident that in showing respect for our traditions we are acting responsibly. In a real sense we cannot 'revive' a religion for that is going backwards. What we can do is respect religious traditions and allow them to take us forward into the future. That is all the old ways ever promised they would do" (*For* 268). Melda and Lupe talk of praying in the traditional way and show us that tradition is something that is worked on and maintained. Lakota tradition is dynamic and changing because it operates within a system of interrelations. Individuals determine what constitutes tradition through interaction and debate. People make up tradition in both senses of the word; they comprise tradition and they construct tradition. Deloria further emphasizes that Lakota spirituality belongs to the people and is characterized by spontaneous community activity (*Custer* 125). Consequently, the process of identifying and enacting tradition effects renewal.

Melda and Lupe's account functions in combination with other stories from both the oral and written traditions of the Lakota people. This associative method is grounded in the oral tradition, in that many stories together compose a cultural perspective; Melda and Lupe's account does not provide a definitive "Lakota perspective."[8] The stories that Melda and Lupe tell are part of an oral tradition that draws on "a complex body" of material. In commenting on the Lakotas and Dakotas, in particular, Elizabeth Cook-Lynn (Dakota) asserts that "there is a fairly long list of Dakota/Lakota writers and storytellers as well as a huge body of ritual and ceremony against which everything may be compared" (*Why* 84). Lakota myths, legends, metaphors, symbols, historical persons, and events "form the basis of the critical discourse that functions in the name of the people" (84). All of these elements work together, forming a network of relationships in the Lakota community. These intersections find expression in Melda and Lupe's lives and serve to reinforce family, identity, and tradition.

2

Long Time Ago

MELDA: So what do I say? My name is Melda Jane Runs Along the Edge Red Bear Trejo. My married name is Trejo, and I've been married to Lupe Trejo for forty years now. And I have eleven kids; I lost three boys. I was born here in Allen, South Dakota. I was born four miles east of Allen.

And my mom came from—she's from Oklahoma. She's a Cheyenne Indian. I'm the seventh generation from my great-grandfathers. My mom and her dad—they came from Oklahoma and she's a Cheyenne, so I'm part Cheyenne and Sioux. And I'm part Mexican because my great-grandma is a Mexican. Her name was Luisa Martinez Runs Along the Edge. And they call her Shell Woman. Her Indian name. She goes by Shell Woman. And I come from a good family. A real nice family. There was no alcohol or they hardly smoked either so. . . .

And in my generation . . . I was born here but I wasn't raised here. I went to school here for a while but I went mostly in Denver, Colorado, and Scottsbluff, Nebraska. When I was a teenager, we would go to Denver in the winter because there was little work in South Dakota. We make little drums and tepees and all kinds of souvenirs. That was a pretty good job. We paint designs. You start out copying someone and you do hundreds and hundreds of those and then come up with your own design. But, then Denver was getting too big. So we moved to Scottsbluff. Probably in 1954. We stayed there. It was like a home to us.

And then we moved back to South Dakota when my mom got real sick. Somewheres around 1989 and '90. We moved back with the kids. My mom asked me to take care of her and she owns quite a bit of land out there, down four miles east of Allen. So I came back and we moved down there and we lived in a tepee for a while. About two years. Because the log house wasn't fit to live in there. There was no electricity so we lived in a tepee for about two years and then they fixed that house up. The log house. And they added two rooms. So that log house is pretty old now. Close to one hundred years old.

And we moved back and my husband got into Sun Dancing. And we got into this Lakota religion. And we try to help people from there. We worked with two medicine men. One of them was Ruben Fire Thunder and when he died we went to Earl Swift Hawk. And we just have sweats. And we learn a lot from Earl and Ruben. And when they both—when he died and Earl's kind of getting old—so we just kind of pick it up. And my husband's really a strong believer that way; in the Lakota ways. And we try, we try to help people out and a lot of times we put a lot of our time and everything into this Sun Dance and we try to help people out and the kids. Through all this Sun Dancing, we experience good things.

My brother, Albert, was the oldest. And, he knew some things. He was older and he knew my great-grandparents, Philip Runs Along the Edge and Luisa Martinez. This was down east at the house in South Dakota. At that time, my dad used to have a lot of horses. A lot of horses. And they had a big corral where we have our garden. My brother said to me, "When I was young they always send me to get the horses. And, I always wonder why." He said, "A long time ago," he said, "with my great-grandma and grandpa," he said, "I was just a boy," and he said, "I remember something when those two old people were alive a long time ago," he said, "and we had a lot of horses," he said, "they always tell me to go after the horses, but I remember something sitting here, too. Those horses they used to come back by themselves early in the morning. Before anybody wakes up and the sun was barely coming. Those two old people get up and they get all dressed up in their traditional ways and that old man used to braid that old woman's hair."

And there is, like, I guess a long time ago when two old people grew old together and when that old woman cannot comb her hair and that old man used to comb the hair. And, you know, they part the hair in the middle and they put red right here in the part in the hair. That *wasa* right in the part. That you use that for the dog. *Wasa*. They put sacred red paint, in English. He said, "Put that *wasa* right there and just braid her hair. And they have a meaning for that, too." And I said, "What's the meaning to put that red hair, red paint right across and comb her hair?" He said, "That means that he loved her very much." Yeah. So that's just like a love story, too. They have that.

But nowadays you don't see anybody doing that, but they used to do that. Those old people. And he talked about that. And he said, "Another thing was that they dressed up in the morning. They get all dressed. And then he sits her down and comb her hair and put the *wasa* and they all get dressed. And those horses would come. Yeah, so they go out and they pray. And all the horses would come. Down east. They all come and they're all around that place. Eating grass. Some are nice. They go out and they talk to the horses and they eat breakfast. She cook. But they was the only two that always eat that breakfast. She cooked and it looks like everything was ready and they were all dressed up nice and they pray. They pray when the sun comes up, they pray. And the horses are there. All those horses. There's about over a hundred of them. They had a lot of horses. And they used to stand around there and they used to go out there and talk to them. Just like, the horses don't take off, they were there. They were there so they go out and they pray and they talk to the horses. And all this was done really early before anyone gets up. So they finish their breakfast and people start getting up and they take their good clothes off and put them away and here those horses take off. And then later on," he says, "They ask me to go after the horses." So, he said, "Why did they ask me, after we have breakfast, 'Go after the horses'?" He said, "I always wonder why."

So it was really like—life was really easy for them. They don't have to catch the horses. They don't have to go after them. They really could control a horse's mind, too. And this brings me up to that *Horse Whisperer*—the movie. Remember the horse got hurt real bad and she had to contact this man who know about the horses. Get inside their mind and they listen. And I was thinking those old people used to do that. They used to get into even the horses and the minds of animals and talk to them. Really gentle. Because they were like that. They were gentle people. They were not—you compare all that to now where we live and it's not the same. Our world is really different from what they were living in those days.

My oldest brother, Albert, took the wrong road at one time and couldn't get off the wrong road and that's why he died drinking. But, he knows a lot. Yeah. And we always go after him and say, "Albert, you run the sweat." And he's real happy and he said, "Okay." He always singed this song, *Miye Wakan*. That's the song he *always* sing—never fails. That was his song. Every time he sits in that sweat. After he died, I always wondered why he always sings it. I never ask and I regret not asking him. After he died, I ask someone and they said, "A long time ago they had this medicine woman. And she lived in Kyle. When they used to go see her, she uses Albert to help her out to put that *wakan* altar. She always use Albert to put, you know, good things in there. And that was her song. And they always sing that song. So she teach Albert how to sing that song and he knew from there." That's why. They say, "Because he used to work with *winyan wakan* that's why he sings that song."

He go with my mom to go see this woman in Kyle a long time ago. This is before my brother got married. My brother, Albert, got married to Christine Crow Dog. Somewheres around 1950. That's when we met the Crow Dogs. Christine's the oldest, Delphine, Diane, and Berta and Leonard. We sort of grew up together. I grew up with Berta. At that time, we lived in Alliance, Nebraska. Remember in about 1949, there was a big blizzard. We went to work and we got stuck over there and we couldn't get back. So we all lived in tents, camping. There was a big old camping place over there. So, not only us, but there were a lot of people. And that's where I met Christine's youngest sister, Berta. I used to play with her. And later on, I guess, my brother and Christine was going around. And, they got married down east.

And, you know, I did have a horse one time. There was one birthday. My eleventh birthday. They took me to my aunt's up north, over here. They used to live where that buffalo pasture is. They had a big birthday party. My aunt made a cake. And we had a birthday. And, well, I'm a twin, but my brother died when we were born. So they invite these people, I guess they were related, and here they were twin boys. They invite them. And here they gave me a horse and I was so happy. We had horses, our horses. But I never claim one for my own. So they say they give me a horse and I was really proud. "Oh," I said, "I have my own horse." They brought those horses in. And it was a wild horse! They were wild horses. Their manes were really long. And their tails were dragging. And they looked scary! I said, "No, Dad, I'm not going to ride those horses. Not *those* horses. They're wild." My dad said, "Well, they're going to break that horse for you." So they did. So I had to wait, like, one year. And they took that horse. It looked like a palomino.

So we came back and I don't know how long, but I think it was about one year later. They brought the horse. My dad said, "You get on that horse and if you fall don't go crying, you get back on there." First time I got on that horse, I fall, I don't know how many times. Boy, did I fall! But, when I fall off the horse, I didn't want to cry. I didn't cry because what he told me. I just had to get back on. And I keep doing that and I do that all summer. I had that horse a long time. And he was really nice. And, you know that horse, I talk to that horse. And that horse really listened. Years later, I used to have a cousin that lives up there, on that hill, and she got into an accident so she was on crutches, she can't walk. And she always tell me, "Come after me, because I want to play with you." I said, "Okay." About that time, that horse really listens to me. He does anything I tell him to do. So my mom used to say, "Go after her. She wants to come and play. She's probably tired of being there." Because she couldn't walk. So I go up there, but I say, "How am I going to bring her down here? I cannot carry her up to that house." And my mom told me, "You'll know what to do. Just go after her. You'll find a way to get her on the horse." So I went up there and I told her, I said, "I came after you to take you down there so we can play." So she comes out with her crutches and she can hardly stand up. And I looked at her and I said, "How am I going to put you up here?" And I said, "I know!" So I got off and I told my horse, "Lay down." And, you know, the horse did! They were really surprised. Her mom and her uncle came out: "Gee, how'd you do that?" So, I said, "Well, I talk to my horse and my horse listens." So the horse lays down and she gets on top and the horse stands up. And that's how I used to bring her down. So I used to bring her back and when I get to the house with her I used to tell the horse, "Lay down." So he lays down. Real gentle. And then she used to get on. So my mom said, "See, I know you'll find a way. The horses, they listen."

So, see, like when Albert talk about my great-grandparents talking to the horse and then they always tell them, "Come back tomorrow." So they did. Every morning. And they do that every morning. But, somewhere along when we was growing up, I know that now we don't use all that. So I think we lost a lot of our traditional ways that they used to do. We lost all that. Because of all this fast living. Even cooking nowadays. So we lost all that. And if we bring all that back it would be really nice. So it's hard . . . really hard. It's hard being patient. As a mother I learn how to be patient. And as a grandma, I learn how to be patient.

LUPE: As a wife?

MELDA: As a *wife*, I learn how to be patient!

LUPE: Well, my dad come from Aztec nation, Aztec tribe. From Old Mexico. Silao, Guanajuato. In the mountains. It's like a little village, a town, with big mountains surrounding. There are seventeen tribes of Aztecs. Seventeen of them. So far as I know. And my father came from there, you know. A long time back. When he was a young boy. He was a young boy when he came to the United States with his father. And he went to Coleman, Texas. They were coming through to North Dakota when they pay a nickel to pass into another state. They pay a nickel apiece. Then they come to Nebraska. They stay there for a while. Him and his father. And his father took off and abandoned him. Forgot about him. Took off. He never see his father no more.

My father raised himself. He was about ten years old. And he fed himself in Nebraska for a while. Scottsbluff. Then he went to Mitchell. I think I've got some relatives over there in Torrington, Wyoming. My grandfather, I think, got married again. Another family. And my father came to Texas. As a young man, there. And met my mother. They got married. They got married and my father never went back to Mexico no more. He stayed right there. With my mother. And they start having us kids. And he has a job, you know. He was working the railroad for many years. Thirteen years. And he came from a tribe of Aztecs. Aztecs from way down deep in Mexico. In the middle. Middle of Mexico. About eight hundred kilometers from the capital city. Mexico City. About a six-hour drive. My father believe in the Catholic and the traditional, but he was a Catholic really. Strong man.

Well, anyway, when I was growing up, you know, I worked on a farm. In the fields. In Texas. Picking cotton. And then we came to Nebraska. Work on the beans and potatoes. And when we're done, we go down to Oregon. Go to Oregon. And I worked in a factory. I was young. I was about fourteen, fifteen years old. I went with my folks. My family. We drove together. And we worked there for about six months. And I work. After I get done, we go back to Nebraska and finish up. And then we travel to Arizona. So it was like that every year. My mom never did work. She cooked for us. She took our breakfast out to us out in the field. About nine o'clock she come with that breakfast. We sit down right there in the middle of the field and eat. Everybody.

I only went one year in school. Not all the way either. Third grade. They put me in third grade. I went to first grade and they put me in third grade because I was too big. With the little ones. So they put me in third grade and I didn't know nothing about it. Nothing about it. Went back to work. I know how to read. I understand the words and all that. I learned that on my own by reading comic books! I learn that by myself. That's why I don't know how to write. Just my name. I never wrote a letter myself in my whole life.

When I was young, you know, I used to go to church with my

mother. And after that, you know, growing up, I was in a seminary. In Texas. Seven years I was there. I thought I might be a minister or Catholic preacher. Seven years in Lubbock, Texas. I was trying to be a regular preacher. I stayed there with the fathers. When it get wintertime a lot of people come and we give them bread, cans of food, you know—gallons, big gallons like that. Like soup, you know. All that. A loaf of bread. Four or five loaf of bread to each. And I do that all the entire day. Every day, I do that. In a church, yeah. In a seminary. A very big seminary. Nothing but men there.

And then one time I just walk away. I went to Coleman, Texas, where my father and mother was. I went back to the seminary one more year. But, after that, I worked there in Texas every year. I decide it might be better to just do it myself. And I didn't pray. I work and work. I never went to church anymore. I work. I came to Nebraska with my folks. Fort Collins, Colorado. I worked there back and forth.

And one year. In 1957. I met Melda. I was about nineteen when I met her. I wasn't praying no more; I didn't go to church no more. Didn't pray or nothing. Not one time. And then I got married . . . well, we stayed together for twenty years before we got married. So I walk away from the religious. I walk away. And . . . I started drinking. But, I worked every day. Every day. Sundays, too.

And, you know, now I tell you about that eagle—it changed my whole life. I was working and one time I went to work early in the morning. Sunday morning. And I had a six-pack of tall boys here. And I was drinking early. And I told Melda, "I'm going to work now." And she said, "Okay. When you come back, I'll have food for you." So I left. I go about four miles. Maybe three. Check my water. Get out of my pickup. And it was a really sunny day. Early in the morning. Sunday. And I seen a big shadow. And right beside me was a big eagle. Really big one. Like three feet high. Big one! Huge! Biggest one I've ever seen in my whole life. And I know he wants to tell me something. And me, I want to *kill* it. I got up and he went like this and jump up and jump down. Jump up and jump down. But then he really scared me. He turned his head all the way around. Like an owl. And his eyes turned color. I was staring at her and she was staring at me. And then it opened its mouth and started saying something to me. But I got in my pickup and took off. Went home. I didn't drink that beer or nothing like that. I let them spill. I got home and Melda said, "You done working?" And I said, "That eagle was bothering me." Melda says, "What eagle?" And I said, "Get in. I'll show you." It was still there. Stayed there four days. Melda's father know. Melda's mother know. And Melda. Went to see it. Four days. Nobody see it. Only us. It was right there. It was by the road. By the lake. On Sunday, a lot of people go back and forth. But they never seen that eagle though.

And it was that day when everything turn my life around. Like somebody came to me and tell me, "You need to pray." And, so I told my boss that I was going to take a week off. And he said, "Okay. I understand that." So I came home. And, later, I told Melda, "Pack up. We're going to leave. We're going to Sun Dance." She was surprised: "What?!?" We went up to Leonard Crow Dog. He was real young. We were young. And I do things that I never done before. You know, pray by the tree. And I pray there. People came to me and asked me if I knew what I was doing. And I said, "Yeah. This year I'll be here with you dancing." I did that for fifteen years. I danced with them.

My mother went to Sun Dance at Leonard's the first year when I danced. I seen her out there. She faint right away and Leonard comes and doctors her. And I told my mother, "Sorry, Mom, I cannot help. Ho! I'm all tied up!" My father was Catholic. He never come for years. But one time I was dancing and I was facing south. My father was against it. He thought I was doing something wrong. And I talked to him. I never argued with my father. So, one time, one year, I was dancing. My mother was there. My father was never around. We went to take the pipes. All of us. I was offering the pipe and I see a person over there, my father. Standing over there. I went over to speak to him. He said, "You know what, son? I'm really happy that you're doing this. I thought you were doing something ugly. I thought you were doing something else." And he liked it. It made me feel real good. He went to the Sun Dance all by himself from Scottsbluff. And, so I start praying in the traditional way, a good way, that's thirty-three years. See, I like to pray this way. I like the way it is. You know, what really keeps me going is my family and people that go ahead and pray in the Sun Dance and the sweat. That's people keeping it strong. People keeping it strong.

3

They Come from the Family

MELDA: I went to school when I was about six or seven. I was raised in Lakota language. I always talk Indian when I was a girl. There was no other language. And, I'm glad I learned the Indian language. When I went to school, it was hard for me to learn English! We were all *Indian* and we talk Indian and we didn't know how to talk English. Oh, I had a hard time learning English in school. My cousins and me went to school. I think the teachers were really having a hard time with us. It took me all that school year and then I started to speak English real good.

In school they teach us how to sew. Clothes. We did our own clothes too. We learn how to run a machine at an early age. Make long skirts. And I think that was pretty good because we didn't have extra clothes, you know. That school was in Allen. American Horse Day School. That old school. We used to stay over there. A lot of us have to walk a half a mile so we have to stay in school. The basement. They call it boarding. We go on Monday and come back on Friday. When we go on Monday and Thursday night we take our showers and wash all our clothes and put them in a suitcase and then we come back and do the same thing. So my mom don't have to wash clothes for us. We learn all this at an early age.

When we're home from school, we come back we have to go to that creek and get our buckets of water and put water in that woodstove. And we wash our own clothes. I get ten pairs of socks, that's it for school and I have to take care of them. In our spare time, my mom always give us little pieces of material to make our own quilt. We don't get bored, you know. We have to make quilts or do *something*. So I make my quilt after school when I get my chores done. We would make a big quilt. Cut it out and then piece it together. So that takes all winter. Come home from school and sit there and do it by hand. The quilt we make was just a block quilt. Squares. People used to make the blocks. Now, they're all fancy! We always talk about how we should make blocks, too. And bring that back. So it would be nice for the kids so they wouldn't have to worry about star quilts. Star quilts are fancy. They're hard to make!

One thing I never did was make bread. Just peel potatoes. The easy part. Wash dishes. I learn frybread, but, oh, frybread came much much later! My mom was always making bread. Good. Soft. In my days, we didn't have a lot to waste. What you have, you're really grateful for. You don't waste food. I try to do that now. Put up a cellar. And can food. And I try to teach my grandkids that.

When I was growing up down east, it was real nice because we just stay down there. I was telling my grandson Paul, I said, "When I was growing up here," I said, "I never get to go town. Just my dad. Go off for food. Like every month." The only time we went to town was on Christmas. One of us goes to Martin with our parents and gets Christmas presents. And we make all our ornaments ourselves. So we'd start two weeks ahead—a month before Christmas. Bring everything home. And we even make those popcorns with that string. We did all that. And even those candy bags we do. We buy some material and make a bag. So mostly everything we have to do that way.

The Lakota way is that you really respect your brothers and sisters. Not even to call them by names: "Say 'brother' in Indian." "Say 'sister' in Indian." So that was the way we was raised. My father sit us down and told me, "Don't play with Norman. He's your brother, respect him." Same thing with Norman: "Respect your sister. You don't tease your sister." And my dad never argued with my mom. I never hear bad words from my dad and my mom. They never argued. They sit us down and they talk to us. And, you know what? A lot of those things are still with me. I really respect my brothers. And I was always taught that. I was taught that way. Up to this day, I never talk back to them. We just sit down and talk real good. So I think my dad's teaching was real good.

Lupe and me both come from strict families. Really strict. But, I never got spanked. They just always talked to us. When we argue, my father sit us down and the first thing he'd tell us: "Touch your ears." So we touch our ears. Both of them. "What are they there for?" And we say, "To hear, to listen." He said, "God gave you those ears for one reason. And you use it. Listen." So he talks to us like that. Oh, he made us go through that . . . touch your ears.

And, my mom always say that your brains is still *nunshila*. It means you can't think, you could get mad, you can't think good things. It means you're young. When she talked about your brains as *nunshila*, I always ask her, "What do you mean by that? *Nunshila*?" And she said, "It's like a watermelon. When you have a garden, and you go touch a watermelon and it's still soft inside. They're still soft. Touch the watermelon. And when the watermelon is ripe, you can hit the watermelon and it'll be hard. And it'll be good to eat. And you'll know. That's how it is with your brains. When you're young it's still *nunshila* up here." That's the way she told me. So every time I put a garden in, I go and hit the watermelon and I say, "I wonder if this *brains* is good!?"

Now, I look back and I think I had the best parents. They didn't drink, they didn't argue. There was no drinking and smoking involved. And my grandparents were like that too. They stayed married for a long time. They say, if you catch a bad disease nowadays or something and they say that's hereditary—well, you can get things in a good way, too. A lot of good things I learned from my mom and pass it on to my grandkids. And I hope they pass it down, too!

My mom used to go to ceremonies a lot. *Yuwipi* ceremony. My uncle Poor Thunder. He used to be *yuwipi*, but he was a real strong *yuwipi* person. He never goes around. He lived a medicine man . . . as a life as a medicine man, he lived that life. When he got married, his wife was chosen. He didn't go to meet the woman of his choice. It was the two parents that chose the wife for him. And when they had a baby girl, that was given to them by the *pejuta*, the medicine.

That was my mom's cousin. So in Lakota ways he's my uncle. Uncle Poor Thunder. I knew him and I used to sit at his ceremonies as a little girl. He was really powerful. And I heard that he . . . he smoked that pipe. The White Buffalo Calf Woman pipe that's in Green Grass. He open it and smoke it. Prayed. For the people. So I'm really proud to come from a good family like that.

Howard Red Bear—in Lakota ways, my grandfather—was real strong. He was a scout, an Indian scout. As scouts, they were given flags. We have those American flags. Philip Red Bear's whole flag. And, I think, Isaac Red Bear's flag. My cousin. We have that. But, Howard Red Bear's pipe was sold to a museum. Sold to a museum. I don't know who and I don't know if it's still there. Trying to get that back, too. Smithsonian. In Washington.

So Howard Red Bear was an Indian scout. One time me and my sister went to visit him in that old house, it was pretty clean. Really neat. He's always having soup. He's always having bone soup. And big crackers. Yeah. We went over there and he said, "Well, granddaughters, I've got soup going." So, we said, "Okay." He had all these army coats and jackets, the big ones hanging there. So when we walked in there we said, "What are you doing with all your army coats? You should throw them away or, you know, burn them. You've had them hanging there for a long time." He said, "No." He said, "They're really warm. To use them for winter." He was a scout and when they have that massacre, Wounded Knee Massacre, he said, "They didn't let us go in. The army told us to keep back." He was talking about that. I remember that story. When me and my sister went over there. And after, he said, "Well, we're going to have some soup!" We sit down and have some soup with him.

He was born in Scottsbluff, Nebraska. He was born at Chimney Rock. Chimney Rock. In Lakota, it's a kind of a word that we cannot pronounce, cannot say. It's a marker. It used to be a marker right there on the maps. It's a marker. When you're traveling. And he was born right there. So that's his birthplace. He tell us about that. He said, in his days, they were traveling and they stopped there and they went to hunt for food. The ladies were supposed to wait there while they went hunting. So his mom stayed there and they all left to hunt food. And, then, *that's* where she had my grandfather. He was born there. That's his birthplace. So I guess a long time ago they don't go by what month the birthdays is. They don't use the month. They go by, like, the trees or the berries. I guess that's how they tell the month, what month they're born. It's really interesting. We ask him, "So when's your birthday?" He said, "When the plums are ripe, I was born." So we figure about August. Yeah, so me and my sister used to go down there and we taste the plums and when it's nice and ripe we used to run to my grandfather and tell him, "Grandfather, it's your birthday now!"

And, you know, there's a lot of stories. My mom come from I guess . . . my mom's grandfather was a medicine man, too. Which I never knew him. They never told me his name. He was very powerful. So . . . we come from medicine. Our ancestors are medicine men.

And, my dad helps people. My dad was a Native American Church minister. But he never did take money. He helps people. And I hear a lot of my nephews and my brothers who say, "I walk in his shoes." He was a nice man. Nice man. He never drinks. He was with my mom for a long time. I think forty years when he died. And then my mom just stayed by herself. And that's the way the Red Bears, the Runs Along the Edge they believe . . . traditional way.

My mom's dad is Philip Slow Dog. And the mother is Mary. But, you know, that my dad's grandparents they had the same name. That's Philip Red Bear. And the wife is Mary. They both have the same name!

My father's dad had only one wife. But Philip had three wives, they say. And they say that when he was down east, where we live now, he was swimming in that water where the grandkids swim. And he was swimming with his three wives. That's when this Catholic father came down the hill with his Bible. On a horse, carrying his Bible. And he saw them three and he told them, "You're supposed to have only one wife, because if you have three wives you're living in sin." He told him, "You have to only choose one." So I guess he choose Luisa. So they said when he choose Luisa he marry down there, you know, where all the kids are swimming, where our water is. The springwater. And he married down there. So these other two women just kind of packed up. They didn't get mad or anything. They just left. With their kids. So he stayed there with Luisa with her kids. The others got married to different men and they keep their kids, that's where I think my uncles are. They have different names but they come from the family.

And, now, you know, I met Lupe in 1957. This is after my family moved to Scottsbluff. So me and Lupe met in 1957. We met when I was fifteen years old. I knew Lupe for a long time. We just run across each other. I always see him—him and his brothers. I was fifteen years old. We always used to go to work in Colorado, in Fort Collins. We went to Fort Collins and he was there. We go somewhere else and he was there! So I knew Lupe for a long time.

When we used to walk uptown, he used to come beside me and he used to ask us for a ride. I met him at a dance—powwow. And, my sister likes to go to Mexican dance. We were young and my mom was really strict. They let my sister go to the dance. So we went over there with her, but I have to sit in the car. So I can watch all those girls' purse. And we had to lock all the doors. Me and my girlfriend. That was Leonard's sister—Berta Crow Dog. I always see Lupe around. And they came over and knocked on the window and they say, "Hey, let us in." And I say, "No, you cannot come in because we're taking care of purses. And you cannot come in."

At the dance, I had a girlfriend that ran away from us. She was supposed to go to this powwow and she was, like, boy crazy, so she took off with a boy. So I was looking for her and that's when I met Lupe. *Again.* He was driving around with his girlfriend! And, I knew this girl. So I told them, "Take us to the powwow." I said, "My girlfriend took off." So they drove me over there. And I couldn't find my girlfriend. So I came back with them. And, you know, things like that. We started getting together. . . .

And then, sometimes he comes around and asks me to go out. And I say, "I can't go out with you because . . ." And, he come back. So we just go drive around. There was no drinking involved. Because my mom was strict. Oh boy, she was strict! So that's how I met him. You know, little by little.

So Lupe came after me to go to Colorado, too. He was going to go work. He asked me if I wanted to go with him. So, I said, "I don't think so." I said, "Because I'm helping my mom out." So my dad told me, he said, "No," he said, "you have your own life." He said, "Someday you're going to have your own life." So I said okay. And I went with him to Colorado. And we worked . . . he worked. And, I just, sort of, clean house; sort of stay home. And it was kind of boring, you know. So, I said, "Well, I think you'd better take me back home." So I came back and stayed with my folks for a while.

And then when he was going to go to Texas, he came after me again. So, I said, "I'll go to Texas with you." So I went to Texas, stayed with him. Off and on like that because I felt I should be helping my parents out. So I was trying to do like both. And I wasn't going to go to Texas, so my dad told me, he said, "Well, you had better go." He said, "Because you have your own life." And again they talked to me.

We came back and Lupe is a Catholic. Strong Catholic. The whole family. And I was like Native American Church—my dad. So we came back and Lupe's mother kept telling us to get married in a church—Catholic church. Oh, I was pushed. It was funny. I thought, "Oh, I'm not a Catholic." I said, "I don't know. Because Catholic is really strict. When you get married you cannot divorce." So I was thinking about that. I said, "If I get married then I'm stuck with him forever! What if I can't keep that commitment?" So, I told Lupe, "I don't want to get married in Catholic. I don't think I can do it." So we talked about it and we said, "Well, we'll wait."

But, they were all pushing us: "You've got to get married." So we went for a blood test. And, they broke our blood! In those days, they don't do it at the clinic right away. They send it to Lincoln. They tell us to come back in one week. So we come back in one week and the nurse said, "Oh, I'm sorry. They broke your blood. You have to do it over." And both of us too! His and mine. You know, that happened four times! Yeah! And the fourth time, I said, "No, that's enough." I said, "I'm going to run out of blood." So we let that go. We never went back. I told Lupe, "No, I think I'm just going to think about being married for a while. I'm all right with the common-law." So I stayed with Lupe for a long time like that. That's why we never got married.

We just stayed together. For the longest time. I say, "We're all right. Common marriage!" So that's what we did. That's why we didn't get married for a long time because they keep breaking our blood. And then I really didn't want to get married in Catholic. You know. But I go to church with Lupe's mom. Every once in a while we go to church. And Christmas, I go to church with her.

We didn't get married until one of my kids, Raymond, was going to get married. They met and I told them to get married because, I said, "You guys are going to have a baby and all that." And that fall back on me that I didn't get married. My mom told me, she said, "Melda, talking to your son like that it's real good." She said, "But did you ever look at yourself and Lupe?" And I said, "Yeah, I know." So we sit there and talk, and she kind of says, "Well, you'd better do something before he gets married." So it didn't occur to me then that getting married was a big thing. So I said, "Okay."

So we get married in Martin. In 1979. We got a blood test again. And, here, they didn't break it! We went to justice of peace in Martin and we got married. Yeah. And all my kids were there. Because they were all born. And they were all happy. So that's what happened. We never got married until 1979. You know, I *stayed* with Lupe for forty years. I wasn't *married* to him. That's a big difference!

But you know what? You know I didn't want to get married in Catholic church? But, then we just did! For our fortieth wedding anniversary. We renewed our vows. There's a little Catholic church down east. I say to Lupe, "We should get married there." For some reason, I like that little church. A lot of my aunts went there. So, I guess, I always wanted to get married there really. And, for some reason, it happened. And, we got married there forty years later.

4

Collaboration

As a non-Native collaborator, my understanding of racial politics has been shaped, in part, by ideals that are characteristic of a post-civil-rights-era mentality. I was born in Toronto, Canada, in 1969 and was educated at alternative public schools before attending university. The broad ideological shifts that accompanied the social movements of that period have influenced my ideas about knowledge and power. Conventional notions of scholarship have been unsettled by indigenous claims, and my own work is an attempt to respond to those claims. Most significantly, in *Custer Died for Your Sins* (1969), Vine Deloria Jr. (Dakota) writes: "The massive volume of useless knowledge produced by anthropologists attempting to capture real Indians in a network of theories has contributed substantially to the invisibility of Indian people today" (86). Deloria's main concern has been that academia is largely irrelevant to the needs of Native communities. The "cultural leave-us-alone" policy presented by Deloria and other Native critics and activists challenges anthropologists to rethink their relationship to Native communities.[1] Anthropologist Elizabeth Grobsmith says that "[t]hose of us 'raised on Deloria' have had built into our knowledge of our discipline issues of ethics and morality, legality and property, jurisdiction and self-determination" (45). Peter Whiteley echoes this sentiment in *Rethinking Hopi Ethnography* (1998): "I was 'raised' more directly on Ortiz than Deloria in this regard but the ethical implications were equally clear" (22). Likewise, I question the ethics associated with what has largely been a colonial endeavor, and I bring these principles to my work in the Native community.

Both Native and non-Native activists and theorists advocate ethical practices, but the shared goals are often elusive. Specifically, post-modernism in anthropology has been associated with critiquing the anthropologist as author, acknowledging biased interpretations, and deconstructing theoretical assumptions. Dakota writer and critic Elizabeth Cook-Lynn notes similarities between postmodern theorist Edward Said's *Culture and Imperialism* (1993) and the views of Dakota scholar Vine Deloria Jr. (*Why* 71). Said and Deloria are both concerned with decentering dominant power structures and practices. Efforts to revision academic practices have also, however, often replicated extant difficulties. For example, the continued struggle to achieve good practices was exemplified at the 1998 Biennial Native American Conference in Boise, Idaho. A well-intentioned non-Native panelist asked, "How can we treat our informants with more respect?" Vine Deloria Jr., who was also on the panel, responded: "If you want to treat them with respect, then stop calling them 'informants.'" Ironically, I found this moment of continuing ethical crisis encouraging; Deloria's observation validated for me that there *are* other ways to conceive of such relationships. "Getting" information from Native "informants" involves being in a position of power as the "knower." As Asha Varadharajan says about research: "There is a false collapsing here of epistemology and appropriation. To know is not always to violate" (qtd. in Hoy, "Thief" 25). Knowledge is associated with power only inasmuch as it replicates the dominance associated with being an "all-knowing" academic; to know everything appropriates knowledge that is not "ours."[2]

Questions about representation have been debated in the Lakota and academic communities around several key texts.[3] Significantly, the collaborative life story *Black Elk Speaks* (1932) is the source of many debates about how to effectively represent Native storytellers.[4] Cook-Lynn describes *Black Elk Speaks* as "the story of an Oglala holy man told by a University of Nebraska poet, John Neihardt" ("How" 79). When Neihardt revealed that he had written parts of the Black Elk text himself, critics questioned the degree to which the material could represent Lakota beliefs.[5] These debates continued in the 1980s and 1990s with postmodern concerns over voice and representation: "In contemporary Lakota public life (e.g. journals, radio shows and public rhetoric) references are frequently made to 'Black Elk's teaching.'

[However, a]nthropologist William K. Powers dismisses the book and its likes as 'the product of the white man's imagination.' He goes on trying to establish the unauthenticity of the book as a document on Lakota religion" (Kurkiala 31). At the same time, several critics and writers, both Native and non-Native, continue to appreciate Black Elk's life and story despite, and even because of, Neihardt's role.[6] Black Elk and his family have not voiced any objections to the collaboration, as demonstrated most recently in *Black Elk Lives: Conversations with the Black Elk Family* (2000), which includes interviews with John Neihardt's daughter, Hilda Neihardt, and Black Elk's granddaughters, Esther Black Elk DeSersa and Olivia Black Elk Pourier. Additionally, Deloria specifically responded to concerns over the veracity of the text in his introduction to the 1979 edition of *Black Elk Speaks*:

> Present debates center on the question of Neihardt's literary intrusion into Black Elk's system of beliefs and some scholars have said that the book reflects more of Neihardt than it does of Black Elk. It is, admittedly, difficult to discover if we are talking with Black Elk or John Neihardt, whether the vision is to be interpreted differently, and whether or not the positive emphasis the book projects is not the optimism of two poets lost in the modern world and transforming drabness into an idealized world. Can it matter? The very nature of great religious teachings is that they encompass everyone who understands them and personalities become indistinguishable from the transcendent truth that is expressed. So let it be with Black Elk Speaks. That it speaks to us with simple and compelling language about an aspect of human experience and encourages us to emphasize the best that dwells within us is significant. Black Elk and John Neihardt would probably nod affirmatively to that statement and continue their conversation. It is good. It is enough. (xiv)

While the tendency to determine what counts as "correct" or "authentic" can be regarded as reductive, these efforts have been a necessary part of considering worldviews and their accompanying ideologies from different perspectives. I had first engaged with debates over authenticity in 1995 when I wrote about *Lakota Woman* (1991) and *Ohitika Woman* (1994). These books are the consecutive coauthored life stories of Mary Brave Woman, also known as Mary Crow Dog and Mary Brave Bird, a mixed-blood Lakota woman from the Rosebud Reservation in South Dakota.[7] I was interested in *Lakota Woman* because it provided information about spirituality from a woman's perspective and from a cultural perspective that differed from my own. Through the process of research and writing, I learned to differentiate among mainstream feminism and women's perspectives associated with different cultures, although we will soon see how this understanding continued to shift. Concerns over authorship and representation, in the eyes of some scholars, undermine the acceptance of *Lakota Woman* and *Ohitika Woman* as "ideal" ethnographic or literary texts.[8] Most notably, Julian Rice critiqued the authenticity of *Lakota Woman* in "A Ventriloquy of Anthros: Densmore, Dorsey, Lame Deer, and Erdoes" (1994). He critiques the role of editor Richard Erdoes, who is an artist from Vienna. He argues that Erdoes constructed much of the text from ethnographic accounts. I only briefly refer to Rice's argument, and to concerns over voice and representation more broadly, because the debate cannot be resolved. Additionally, Mary Crow Dog herself has not objected to Erdoes's manipulations of the text. She stresses that making the information known is more critical than authorship concerns (Wise and Wise). Initially, in my own collaboration I had thought that the genre of life history would resolve postmodern concerns over the cultural biases of mediated accounts by offering an "authentic" account. Instead, I came to understand that all accounts are mediated in some way and that the best approach might be to instead learn from that mediation.

In 1996, when I went to Pine Ridge Reservation with the specific idea of collaborating, I had wanted to work with a Lakota woman who could tell me about women's roles in Lakota spiritual practices. Clearly, I had an agenda and was, unintentionally, seeking out an "informant." I also had ideas about what constituted a "good" informant. I only considered individuals who were readily identifiable to the non-Native community as "being Indian." More specifically, I wanted to work with someone from a prominent family who had recognizable status in both Native and non-Native communities. However, my ideas about what constitutes authority began to shift as I learned more about the community. John Beverley says that "[p]ower is related to representation: which representations have cognitive authority or can secure hegemony, which do not have authority or are not hegemonic" (1). Accordingly, I had to shift what I regarded as important, what mattered, to understand power differently. By listening to Melda's stories and learning more about Lakota culture, I recognized different ways of conceiving power in the Lakota community.

Initially, I had considered that any dislocation from the reservation would mean that an individual might somehow be "less Indian." Melda has lived in Texas, Arizona, Colorado, and Nebraska as well as on Pine Ridge Reservation. She outlines how she has been separated from the reservation community at times in her life, and she talks about her slow and gradual decision to move back to Allen. At the same time, she clearly states, "I was born here in Allen, South Dakota." She articulates her identity by associating her own life with the history of the Lakota people and their connection to the Pine Ridge Reservation. That history has necessarily been contested; the Lakota people have been subjected to significant restrictive government policies. In this context, specifically, the Wheeler-Howard Act, or Indian Reorganization Act of 1934, promoted elected tribal governments but also contributed substantially to increased poverty (DeMallie, "Legacy" 130). Consequently, Melda, who was born in 1939, describes her family leaving the reservation to find work. She simply describes her life; she does not refer to the government policies that make her experience more understandable to me. Accordingly, it took me some time to see that her family's migrations in and outside of the reservation reflect a particular history, one that involves confinement—the parceling of land and other colonial practices—and one that is distinctly "Indian."

When we began our collaboration, I initially failed to include Lupe in the project—one of my most significant missteps. This was by no means necessarily a conscious decision, but it was one that I came to understand later on. At the outset I had conceived the entire project in ways that privilege mainstream feminist views. From my perspective as a non-Native feminist, I had thought that I should focus solely on Melda's life story. My tendency to privilege women's experiences was reinforced by familiarity with feminist interpretations in anthropology that regard gender differences as significant, namely, that Native men and women provide different accounts, that these accounts are best interpreted without gender bias, and that it is often socially inappropriate for a woman to work closely with a man (Cruikshank et al. 3, 19). I had suggested to Melda that we record *her* life story, and I had not considered Lupe's role. The first two recording sessions involve only Melda. Lupe interrupts these sessions several times. He comes in to look for his keys, to listen, to ask questions, and to call us for dinner. At one point Melda talks about groceries, and he corrects her, saying that it should be "food," not "groceries." Then, later, he comes in to tell us that he has finished cooking dinner and says, "The kids are going to eat me up!" Lupe surreptitiously and persistently disrupts the "girl talk," presumably in an effort to expand my conception of the project. Melda probably also made delicate suggestions before she formally requested that Lupe be included. After our initial recording sessions in November 1997, at Melda's suggestion, Lupe was included in the project.

I have personal and cultural biases and can never ultimately know what qualifies as "right" or "wrong." However, disclosure as to what I regard as "right" or "wrong" promotes cross-cultural understanding. I attempt to be reflexive, or "conscious of being self-conscious," and to use the ideas that come from my learning process to continually revise my own interpretations (Goulet xxxix).[9] Here, my tendency to focus on men and women as distinct is grounded in my mainstream feminist beliefs. I came to recognize that cautions about cross-gender communication in fieldwork are not necessarily universal.[10] And, I began to understand that there might be different ways of conceiving of gender and authority and, therefore, different ways of conceiving of the project. Family, with an emphasis on *encompassing* gender roles, serves as the main organizing principle in the lives of Melda and Lupe. It is therefore necessary that they recorded their lives together, and I certainly would not have learned the same thing from Melda's stories alone. Vine Deloria says that "stories must be passed along as part of the family heritage in the same manner as physical goods" (*For* 184). In this sense, the *tiyospaye*, or kin group, is central to the support of the community. Accordingly, identity, family, and tradition are connected in ways that *align* Melda and Lupe and their stories, and this was one of the first significant lessons that I learned in our project together.

5

We Started Getting Together

LUPE: My mother was a good woman. She doesn't speak English. She talk nothing but Mexican. Melda learned a lot of Mexican from her. Because she never tried to speak English. She was always talking Mexican. And, my mom has never been to Mexico. She was born here. Born in Coleman, Texas. And, my mother is part English. My grandfather was a man who was tall, light complexion, blue eyes. My grandmother was kind of little, dark, with black eyes. But my grandfather was white, you know. Light complexion, blue eyes. I've got four cousins—two boys, two girls—who have green eyes. Really green eyes. It comes from the English side, you know. There's an old picture of my grandma. My mother's mother. Dressed like a white woman. A long time ago when they had those hats. And a dress like the white woman. In the olden days.

My mother was always there for us all the time. She had a hard life taking care of us kids. There were about eleven of us all together. When we do something bad, she talk to us. And all that. My mother she liked to pray a lot. Every morning. My mother was a nice woman. She never said no to nobody. She had a soft heart. If somebody get hurt, she cries. But, my mother also has the bloodline of the English and they get mad right away. She's a nice lady, but don't get her mad. She was that kind of woman. Felt things hard. She'd cry for anything. She'd cry for anything. But once you get her mad, that's it. She would use a knife! And, well, my father had a hard heart. *Hard.* He was strict. Sometimes he got real mad. But, if you talk to him, and sit there and then, finally, he gives in. You've got to go through him and then he comes around to your reach.

My father never picks up papers from Mexico. He never had papers. One time, in Texas, they were arresting people. The war was on. And my father volunteer. He was going on a train. But, this time they turn him back because the war was over. So he never got to go. He was supposed to fight. He was going that way. But as a volunteer. Not a drafter.

When we were growing up, we travel a lot from Texas to Nebraska, to Texas again, and then back to Arizona. On different farms. When the winter arrives, we've got to make money, you know. So we get enough money, finish all the work for the farmers and then we drive back home to Coleman, Texas. And we stay there and my father works on the railroad. For thirteen years, he worked on the railroad. I still remember to this day that he used to go to work and he stays away from us every fifteen days. Every fifteen days he comes. He bring all the money. He stay at the house for fifteen days and he make sure he buy everything. Plenty of groceries. Bacon. Salt pork. They hang it up, you know. And then the train comes by and pick him up and bring him to the station. He worked like that all his life.

We were working ourselves in Coleman, Texas. We were working on a farm. Except Sunday, you know. My father was a strong believer that Sunday was for the Lord's Day, you know. He never works on Sunday. He said, "Never work on Sunday. That's the day for the Lord." He believe in the Catholic. And, my brothers and sisters work. We were all working. And all that money goes to my father and mother. But there was a special day. Every Saturday. He says, "Sons, daughters. Today's Saturday. What you earn today, you keep. The more you work, the more money you'll make." We'd make more money that day than the whole week! We work that special day and buy things. I got two guns, caps, and a hat. All-round American. They teach us how to earn our money. All week long, you know, until Friday we work for the family. For food. For clothing. When I would get my money, I would get a whole bag of candy. And a bottle of pop! RC in a bottle. And, go to a movie!

My father was working for John Wayne's ranch, too. He goes in the house, he clean around the stables, and do all the gardening, cutting all the grass around there and all that. So he got to meet John Wayne. Many times. He said he was a nice man to talk to. Really polite. And all that, you know. So that's the way my father got to meet John Wayne in real life. He was a good man. Work on a horse ranch. He was a real nice man to work for. He worked there for a long time.

My father had a truck too. A big truck. He had a lot of customers. And we're the ones behind the truck, you know. Helping out. Putting the bags of potatoes in. He's the driver. He'd pay us for four hours in the back. Two on each side and the other one on top. They're big potatoes, you know. Big sack like this. Pick it up and put it in the truck. Stack it. We do that all day. Ten until midnight. Sixty pounds from the ground to way up here. And I was the shortest one. I'd tip over!

My father had a lot of money. He had lots of money. A car every year. He always had money. And he make sure the family was okay. Not just thousands, but *a lot* of money. And he rented a house. Even if he's not working, his rent was paid for that year. He was a man who never asked nothing from nobody. A big pride on him.

My father try really hard, you know. But something happened to him, you know. He turned out to start drinking real bad. He was drinking a lot and he turned out to be a bootlegger! He was a bootlegger. He tried to provide for us, you know. *More*. We had a good life but he wanted more. So he went to jail. He got into jail and it cost a lot of money. Everything he had saved, he had to pay. And that turned out to be no good at all. So that's no more of that bootlegging. He quit that.

My father, you know, he likes to have his good times too, you know. And he comes around and he dances in Indian and Aztec. He dances Indian for us. Talk to us in Indian. In Indian—Aztec. And dance. Play around with us. Coming Monday, he was a new man again and gets to work. My father believed in the Bible. And he teach every one of us the Bible. He sit the boys and the girls around and my mother and he read to us. Every night that he was home. Every night. And he was a full-blooded Aztec.

My father was strict with us. But he was a good man. When he say something, he live by that. He never change his word. He teach himself all those things because his father left him when he was young, you know. Nobody raised him. Raised himself. He thought what he was doing was the right thing, you know. To be strict with us because he never had a father to be strict with him. My father tried real hard. Sometimes I think he tried too hard, you know. Again I tell you that, because I knew that my father tried to walk two roads. He sat down and told us one time, he said, "Son, don't be like me. Don't fall in this hole where I have fallen, because it's really hard to get out." See, he was talking about his drinking: "Don't fall in this hole, because it's really hard to get out." And, now, to this day, I know what he means. When you start something like smoking, like myself, it's hard to quit. And I see a lot of people drinking and it's hard to stop. That's what he meant.

MELDA: Our first children were born in Coleman, Texas. We used to go to Coleman, Texas, a lot. We used to travel with Lupe's whole family. And I mean the *whole* family. All the cousins and uncles. And brothers and sisters. When I met Lupe, just the boys talk English. Not the girls. Lupe's mom, she's not going to talk to you in English. She's Mexican and she's going to *be* a Mexican and she's going to keep her language. Sometimes, I had a hard time understanding. So we travel with the family. In those days, they used to rent a house and they all live in the same house. But, you know, nobody ever argue or fight. We just go to work and come back and we'd be so tired and go to sleep. So work was really important. And saving money is another thing. You have to *save* money. So we used to go back like that. And then we went to Arizona from Texas. We went from Texas to Arizona and back to Scottsbluff. And the next year, it's the same thing.

Yeah, it's just like we're migrant workers so we just followed the season. We used to go from Scottsbluff; we used to go to Texas and then to Phoenix and then we come back to Scottsbluff and stay there and then it starts all over again. And we go to Texas. They used to pick cotton in Texas. I never did pick cotton. It was too hard. You have to drag those sacks. That was a hard job! I did everything but that was a really hard job. In Phoenix, when we went over there we used to pick all kinds of vegetables. All kinds of beans, oranges. We used to pick oranges. We used to go to the orange fields and, oh, I guess we eat a lot of oranges instead of picking them!

And I work with a lot of Mexican people. From Mexico. When we went over there, oh boy, we worked with a lot of people there. Just big families. We worked every day. We have to get up early, too. Because you have to be out in the fields about four o'clock in the morning. You have to be out there and get into boxes or whatever you're going to do. You have to be there early. But it was pretty good. It was like bending down, you know, you've got to bend down and up and down. So we do a lot of field work. And I think that I hate working inside because I'm used to outside. I'm an outside person!

We was going back and forth and finally, one time, we went back and we worked for this Japanese guy in Phoenix and he gave us this really nice house and he told us to go back every year. And that was even better because, you know, we used to go look for houses. But this one he said, "You guys can come back and stay here every year." I said, "This works for me." So that's what we did for, I think, twenty years we went back and come back and that was pretty good money. Oh, we make money! Lots of money!

LUPE: When I first work on a farm, it was before I met Melda. In Nebraska, we came to a town named Sidney. We didn't have a car back then. They pick us up in a cattle truck. From Sidney to Scottsbluff is about forty or fifty miles. I went to work on a farm. There's a man working out there. His name is Dave Martin. He was a good man to work for. He's got everything. Plates, beds, spoons. Everything. There was food in the house. Dave Martin, he's a good man. He's got kids. One named Earl, the oldest one. And the other one named Don. And the youngest one had a daughter named Margie. They had another daughter, named Doris, but she got killed in a car crash. So we grew up with them all our life. Then, I worked for Don for a long time, too. He teach me the tractor. I was real young, you know. I work with him until I was grown up. Up to the time when I met Melda. And, then me and Melda used to work for him when we were young. And then he couldn't afford me no more, he got broke. He told me that: "I'm really sorry. It's been a rough season."

So then I went with another man named Orville and I work for him about six months and then he couldn't afford me either. Those days were really hard. So I work for another man and I work for him for another six months but he was a really bad man, you know. The women were working really hard pulling up weeds—labor, you know. So I showed him my work and he liked it but I told him, "No."

And then I worked for Dale Carrier. Dale. I stay with him thirty-eight years. A long time. He's a good man. That's where I work now. He's one month older than I am. He's sixty years old. So, this man, we grew up with his family. Like my family. Up to this day we know each other. And their sons and daughters. He had three boys named Terry, Ty, and Todd. Terry was a baby when I started working. And now they're all grown up. Men. They've got their own kids.

When they were kids, the boys really like me. They talk to me. They bring me cigarettes, pop—all the time, you know. When I was young and I used to drink. When Terry was young—about ten or eleven—he said, "Hey, Lupe"—sometimes they call me uncle—"Uncle, you want a beer?" "Yeah." And they bring me a beer. And now he's got boys, kids, and they call me "Grandpa." They call me "Grandpa." A little boy like that: "Grandpa Lupe." I'm really proud when they call me like that. So we all grow up together.

His farm is about a thousand acres. We did beets, corn, alfalfa, and beans, and that's it right there. Me, I ride my eighteen-wheelers. Combines. Caterpillars. Graters. Tractors. All that I know how to do. I taught myself, you know, because I needed to. I ride about everything. I learn all by myself. My boss teach me and I had a good mind and I want to learn and I learn. I learned those things. I've never had an accident. Combines for beets, the corn, the hay. Everything they plant, I plow.

When I started with him, he had one tractor. It was "Nineteen." It's called "Nineteen." Real old tractor. Now, I work with him and he's bought his own farm, got a new house, new tractors, new combines, cattle. A lot of cattle. So he's appreciated my work. Seven days a week. And I work until midnight. Get up at six o'clock in the morning. And then at six o'clock I come in and eat and on Saturdays I tell him I'm going to pick up my check and I get some groceries and my clothes and cigarettes and he'll do that for me. I trust that I'll have everything. Make sure there's everything for the kids. I never get money for *me*. I never say: "This is *my* money." Nothing like that. Never have done that. And Melda knows how to plan it out. I give everything to her and she plans it out. You have a big family, you've got to plan it out!

MELDA: We have a garden every year. Even when my mom was sick. There was a garden there. We have a garden when I was raising my kids in Scottsbluff. We had a garden and we had chickens.

LUPE: A lot of chickens. Five hundred!

MELDA: In spring we ordered five hundred chickens. And we had this big freezer. Because I had all these kids. So when those chickens get to like four months, I dress them up and freeze them. Fryers, we call them. That's mainly what we would get the chickens for. So they go all into the freezer. So I don't have to buy chicken. Same thing with cows.

LUPE: Prepare ourselves for winter, you know.

MELDA: They give us a cow. They give us a whole cow. They process that for us. They bring all those hamburgers and stuff. So that goes in the freezer. Yeah. And a pig. Which we send it out and they always make pork chops.

LUPE: So we always have a garden and we're always preparing food. And we still do that. In other words, you're making your schedule ahead of time.

MELDA: Self-sufficient. So we always have a garden. And then I can tomatoes. Which I don't have to buy tomatoes. And I cook with tomatoes a lot. Everything you put tomatoes in. Chili.

LUPE: You know, many years we travel—me and her. South Dakota— we used to visit there. And then come back. Yeah. And go to Texas.

And work picking cotton. I pick it and she helps a little bit. She helps holding the sack. I hold a sixty-feet sack and I put Robert and those kids on the side and I pull them and pick cotton. We made pretty good money. We had everything.

MELDA: And, I was working sometimes, too. I work at the hospital. I went in for training for cooking, housecleaning, laundry. I like cooking the best. It helped me get a job in Martin. I got me a job in Martin!

And, Lupe paid all his Social Security so we don't have to go through the other ways. Social Security supplements—and that's hard to get. But this way, you pay all your quarters and you get your Social Security.

LUPE: We were people who had everything. The house. New car. Good clothes. And all that. But I seen that we're not happy. We were starting to argue and all that. We had everything. Then we turned to the traditional ways and left everything.

MELDA: For South Dakota. My mom didn't move back down east until after my dad died. That was 1972 when she moved back over here. Then, we used to come back every summer. We worked in Phoenix every winter. In the summertimes, we used to put up concession stands all over the powwows. We always put concession for every powwow. That's how we earned our money in the summertime. The kids liked it and we met a lot of friends and relatives.

And, then later, my mom wanted me to move back to South Dakota. So, I said, "Okay, I'll *try*." I didn't say that I was going to. I said, "I'll try." I said, "Mom, it's too hard, you know. There's no electricity down here!" And I said, "There's no work." You know, when you get paid like every week, you're used to that for so long. You're used to that. Because, you know, I was living in the city. I'm used to that kind of life. When you work, you pay your bills. Makes life easier! But you have to keep working.

When I move back there, it was really hard for me. My grandkids had to take a bath out in the creek. And it was cold for them. We had to warm the water. We had to haul water. We had to live in the tepee. But, that was really cozy. We put carpets in the tepee. And we had bunk beds in there. And we had the stove in the middle. Yeah, you could put a lot of stuff in a tepee!

There was the house there. But, it needed to be fixed. I said to Pine Ridge: "Fix the roof. And I'll move down there." So they did. They came and fixed the roof. So it was alright. One big room. It was alright, it was nice and warm. So we started out like, you know, little by little. And then Pine Ridge came and fixed the whole house and added two rooms and the bathroom. So after they fix that house and we move back in there, it was really nice. We had a bathroom. So then I had to come up with two thousand dollars for that light to go down there. Which I did. I said I'd have to talk to two directors, one from Pass Creek and one from Scottsbluff where we used to live. She made a statement about it over here. So I told them I'll pay my light bills. And, beside that, I'll give you a hundred dollars a month. Until I pay that two thousand dollars. Which they agree. So that's how I got my lights. So that was really good when you have lights.

Oh, but we didn't have TV, because you couldn't get no cable. Can't get nothing down there. It's way down there. So we bought a TV and what we did was we bought a lot of movies. So those kids always watch movies. So we were sort of like coming up with something every year.

But, I never thought I was going to settle down over here. Because I thought I'm going to be in Scottsbluff. I was raised there and I was thinking of just living there. But I keep coming back. We didn't really come back one day and just stay here. We kind of moved back little by little! And then Lupe was having sweats with Ruben Fire Thunder. And, my mom talked to me a lot. And we got involved in this traditional way.

6

Affiliation: Lupe

Academic theorists have questioned the degree to which cross-cultural representation is possible because of the cultural biases associated with interpretive frameworks. Specifically, in "Can the Subaltern Speak?" (1988), literary theorist Gayatri Chakravorty Spivak concludes that the subaltern "cannot speak" because of the differences between Native and colonial discursive modalities.[1] John Beverley elaborates, in *Subalternity and Representation: Arguments in Cultural Theory* (1999), that "[w]hen Gayatri Spivak makes the claim that the subaltern cannot speak, she means that the subaltern cannot speak in a way that would carry any sort of authority or meaning for us without altering the relations of power/knowledge that constitute it as subaltern in the first place" (29). In the foreword to *A Companion to Postcolonial Studies* (2000), Spivak writes: "My endeavor in 'Can the Subaltern Speak?' was to tell the story of Bhubaneswari Bhaduri (and why she could not be heard). . . . Her name is never mentioned in the discussions of my essay" (xxi). With this straightforward assertion, Spivak makes her point: no one heard Bhubaneswari Bhaduri; everyone heard Spivak. As academics, we are hesitant about speaking for others because we are concerned that we will appropriate meaning through misinterpretation; the question is, in effect, "can we hear?"[2]

The suggestion has been made that we can rethink the power relations of "speaking for the other" by substituting any number of alternate prepositional phrases that connote a different relationship: speaking nearby, speaking on behalf of, speaking in place of, or speaking about. All of these formulations in the "identitarian 'speaking for' debates" (Spivak, "Foreword" xviii) have only one speaking subject. "Speaking with," however, denotes two speaking subjects. In an interview, Maria Campbell (Métis) talks about the importance of honoring one's subject position in order to learn from other perspectives: "I know my place and I'm tired of explaining it to people who don't honor their own place and their own history. You don't have to be Native to know what I'm saying. I can tell when I'm reading to a room of people that they know because they honor the things they have. That knowing is an unspoken thing" (Silvera 266). I am privileged to be in a position of learning in hearing Melda and Lupe's stories; that *is* my privilege. Acknowledging white privilege is of little use unless that privilege is regarded in a network of socio-political relations. Most specifically, it is of little use if being "white" and, therefore, "privileged" prevents us from investing in the values associated with research and learning, namely, working toward social justice. If I attend to their perspective of the exchange, I can recognize that Melda and Lupe are speaking to me because they think that I *can* hear. I presuppose that Melda and Lupe, as well as myself, have equally valid perspectives. By bringing these standpoints into rela-tion—by literally and metaphorically talking with each other—we are able to sustain an alliance. We are ultimately speaking with each other about the knowledge we can gain in being allied.

In our collaboration, my tendency to downplay that which might not be readily identifiable as Lakota no doubt contributed to my initial exclusion of Lupe from the project. It further meant that I tended, once he was included, to overwrite his ethnic identity. Specifically, when I initially wrote about Melda and Lupe I characterized them *both* as Lakota. I noted that Lupe was Mexican, but I downplayed qualities that unsettled his association to Lakota spiritual practices. I inadvertently used what Lupe said about Lakota culture to support my own construction of him as an "authentic Lakota informant." I failed to understand his characterization of himself as a Mexican American, supporting multiple identities. In an early draft of this work, those in the academic community pointed out that I tended to label Lupe as "Lakota" despite his own avoidance of such a designation. I reviewed the transcripts of our storytelling sessions and recognized that I had, in effect, overwritten his ethnic identity. I talked about this with the family members who had read the draft, and although they did not feel that I had misrepresented Lupe, they provided me with more information about the Mexican side of the family.

Born and raised in Coleman, Texas, Lupe grew up in an area that has been described as "an extension of Mexico in terms of its Catholic religion, folklore, architectural styles, medium of communications, and cuisine" (De Leon 268). Largely migrant workers, and accustomed to displacement, the Mexican people in this area of Texas cultivate a deep sense of a Mexican American culture, "Tejano" culture (De Leon 268). Nonetheless, Lupe stresses his connection to Mexico and his Aztec ancestors. When I first recorded Lupe, Melda prompted him to start talking about himself and his family. He makes a joke, and we talk at great length about the spelling of the name of the town that his father is from before he finally starts talking about his ancestors in Mexico.[3] The four-page exchange is included here in an edited format:

MELDA: [To Lupe:] Why don't you talk about your dad and where you come from, Lupe?

LUPE [jokingly]: No, I come from my mother. Ho! [laughing]

MELDA: She's recording. So go ahead and . . . You came from your dad's an Aztec Indian and your mom.

LARISSA: That's far back. Aztec. . . .

LUPE: There are seventeen tribes of Aztecs. Seventeen of them. So far as I know. And my father came from there, you know.

Lupe talks about his ancestors in Mexico as well as his connections to Mexican culture and his involvement in Lakota spiritual practices, without ever specifically addressing his *own* ethnic identity. Nonetheless, he is always clear about *not* being Lakota.

Indians have been defined collectively as a group since the colonial era. Consequently, "difference" functions "on both sides of the binary system" (Lionnet 14), and essentialism, or rather the process of "essentializing," is, in this respect, a defensible notion (Paine 92).[4] We can see this affirmation of difference in Lupe's descriptions of his mother. Lupe's maternal grandfather was Caucasian, and I was surprised to learn this because it had never been mentioned before and because Lupe definitely does not come across as "white." He describes his mother's mixed-blood status, but nonetheless he stresses her ties to Mexican culture:

LUPE: My mother is part English.

LARISSA: *Really!* She's like half Mexican, half white?

LUPE: My grandfather was a man who was tall, light complexion, blue eyes. My grandmother was kind of little, dark, with black eyes. But my grandfather was white, you know. Light complexion, blue eyes.

MELDA: So the blue eyes run in the family. Lupe's uncle is really white and has got blue eyes and green eyes.

LUPE: I've got four cousins—two boys, two girls—who have green eyes. Really green eyes. It comes from the English side, you know.

Lupe goes on to say: "My mother doesn't speak English. She talk nothing but Mexican." He implies that, despite his mother's parentage, he considers her Mexican; after all, she speaks only Spanish, or, as Lupe says, Mexican. Melda, who found the language barrier difficult in her conversations with Lupe's mother, emphasizes the connection between language and ethnic identity in describing Lupe's mother: "She's Mexican and she's going to *be* a Mexican and she's going to keep her language." In talking about his father, Lupe similarly stresses a connection to Mexico, namely in his father's connection to Silao, Mexico.[5] He says, "[My father] came from a tribe of Aztecs. Aztecs from way down deep in Mexico. In the middle. Middle of Mexico." This delineates his heritage as distinct from the border towns of Mexico and disassociates his family from the political contingency of the U.S./Mexican border. He describes his father as a full-blooded Aztec who was born and raised in Mexico. He says that his "ancestors from Mexico, they're traditional Aztecs. Indians." In emphasizing a Mexican identity that belies his ancestral history in the United States and maintains ties to the Aztecs, Lupe offsets colonial history and racial categories. He works against the discourses associated with the culture and history of colonization in *both* North America and Mexico.

The Lakota spiritual practices with which Lupe associates his vision of the eagle transform what, for him, has been the distinction between "the Catholic" and "the traditional." He highlights his personal experience of Mexican religious syncretism and indicates that he chose to leave the seminary at a young age. In describing his father, Lupe says, "[h]e believe in the Catholic *and* the traditional, but he was a Catholic really." He notes his father's Catholicism and contrasts the culture associated with colonial Mexico with "the traditional." His descriptions of Aztec culture are stereotypically "Indian," namely involving ritual. Nonetheless, Lupe's story of the eagle resonates with Lakota imagery and symbolism, and he interprets the vision as meaning that he should connect with Lakota beliefs and practices.[6] He specifically chooses this event, rather than other possible contributing factors, as prompting his decision to engage in Lakota ceremony: "And, you know, how I tell you about that eagle—it changed my whole life. And then when I start praying in the traditional way, a good way, that's thirty-three years." He begins to dance at Leonard Crow Dog's Sun Dance and follows the "good red road."[7] He finds comfort in knowing that his father, a Catholic, supports his spiritual beliefs. The description of his parents supporting him at the Sun Dance is one of the most moving parts of his story, and Lakota spiritual practices become a source of transformative power in his life. The eagle dismantles the rift Lupe has experienced in his life—one which dictated that he "walk away from the religious." In this way, Lupe's spiritual experiences in the Lakota tradition promote a resolution around what has been, in his life, the distinction between "the Catholic" and "the traditional."

In Melda and Lupe's lives, the moves toward Lakota spiritual practices have often been initiated through shifts that have occurred in Lupe's life. Most significantly, Lupe made a pivotal decision to break from the behavior that characterized his early years, namely drinking and fighting. It is through Lakota tradition that he made this shift, and he maintained sobriety for the remainder of his life. Having met Lupe in his later years, I cannot imagine him as reckless. I understand, however, that the internal pressures of racism and colonialism can be manifested in dependency on alcohol. Dakota educator Joyzelle Gingway Godfrey explains the connections between alcohol and colonial discourses:

> So lots of "stuff" we're going to have to rethink . . . and think about what we want to be; who do we want to be? Who are we, truly? That's something we need, as Indian people; we need to look at our true history, the reality of who we really were, as human beings, so that we can be human beings, so that we're not trying to live up to those thoughts, pictures, something that we never were. My God, no wonder we have so much alcohol and drug abuse, no wonder we have suicide. Our teenagers are killing themselves in droves—what do they have to live up to? On the one hand, they see their parents, the alcohol and drug abuse that's horrible; on the other hand, they see themselves as supposed to be this noble Indian, you know. So for them there is no middle ground. There is no safety net. Yet there truly is. (qtd. in Gardner 464)

The dichotomized stereotype associated with "Indians"—the noble Indian or the drunken Indian—functions in the erasure of the past and contributes to an overwhelming sense of internalized oppression.[8] The pressures of racism can be felt on a personal level and worked through on a personal level: "Like all people confronted with an oppressive government and racist colonialism, the Sioux are familiar with hatred. It begins with the hatred felt from others and the hatred felt for others, from outsiders, and, then, it sometimes turns into self-hatred, that is, internalized oppression, which eventually, and mercifully, can become the landscape of resistance" (Gonzalez and Cook-Lynn 87).

Breaking from his years of drinking, Lupe moves toward ceremony as a "landscape of resistance." He takes up Sun Dancing and danced for more than twenty years, roughly one-third of his life. Melda and Lupe's story of the Sun Dance is one that spans much of their adult lives. The Sun Dance began in 1988, run by Earl Swift Hawk, and was held in memory of medicine man Ruben Fire Thunder. It continued for three four-year cycles before being dedicated as a memorial Sun Dance in honor of Lupe Trejo. This is the story that Melda and Lupe wanted me to hear: the story of how they came to hold a Sun Dance and how it keeps the family, the community, strong.

PART II

Identity

7

Sun Dance Got Started Down Here

MELDA: Okay, we're going to talk on how we got into the Sun Dance. Lupe talked about the eagle, the eagle that he saw, but the way we also got started on the Sun Dance was when Lupe's mom was real sick. We started to Sun Dance because of Ruben Fire Thunder. We lived in Scottsbluff and Lupe's mom was really sick. And she was going to die. In 1968. The doctor said she's going to die. So all Lupe's aunts came from Texas. This was really sad because the doctor said, "This is her last night. She's not going to make it. She's dying."

So, at that time, my brother, Norman, and Cleo, my sister-in-law, lived in South Dakota, in Allen. You know, my brother is married to Lupe's sister. So they called us. She told me, "Melda," she said, "I don't think that I can lose my mom this year. I can't take that." She said, "We're going to do one last thing for her." She said, "I'm going to send that Ruben Fire Thunder, the medicine man, over there. And they're going to have a ceremony."

So we're supposed to get ready for the ceremony. And, for this ceremony, you need to cook a dog. She told us to look for a dog. And I'd been to Sun Dance and I grew up in a traditional way. When I was young I used to go there to ceremony, but I've never actually cooked a dog and all these things. Yes, I'm there when they eat dog but I've never actually cooked the dog. I've never been through this. So we were supposed to be ready for ceremony in three hours. We were supposed to catch a dog and singe the dog and cook it. It was really hard because when you live in a city, you can't do that! There was no way you were going to start a fire outside in Scottsbluff. Oh we had fun . . . and we got the place ready. We had a ceremony for her that night. And all of Lupe's aunts came over. The aunts speak Mexican, they didn't speak English. So we had a friend there and Lupe was interpreting for his side of the family. Lupe tells our friend in English and then he tells Indian to Ruben. That was three, two interpretation there. So that was really hard. It took us *long*. We spend until like four o'clock in the morning!

Ruben was a real good medicine man. I think that was the first time we met him. So they prayed for Lupe's mom. He said, "They're going to give her one year to live." But he said, "On the same day that next year she'll die." So they extend it one year for her. So, at that time, at that ceremony, Lupe said, "My mom's well and I'm going to go out and *hambleceya*. I'm going to go on top of the hill. Because she's going to live for one year."

When we went to the hospital, she was sitting up! Yeah. They had told me to make *wasna*, *wojapi* and fry bread for her. She was supposed to eat that first. So I walk in there with *wojapi*, fry bread and *wasna*. They don't do that at the hospital. The nurses were surprised. So we explain it to Lupe's mom and she said, "Okay, that's good." She said, "I don't remember anything, but the nurses say that all those IV's and everything they started to shake real bad." They were supposed to put Indian medicine, Lakota medicine, in those IV's. So I guess they did. The spirits did. That's why it was all shaking. Miracles happen. Like that.

So she came and she was doing pretty good and she was out of the hospital within three days, I think. They took her home and she was really happy. So all her sisters they stayed there. They're all from Texas. So after she got better, they all went back. And a year later, she got real sick. She was happy to die. Because I guess she knew. Yeah. When she was in the hospital she was telling her daughters, she said, "Four white horses came after me." She said, "And I'm real happy." She said, "I'm happy to go." And she kind of keeps looking up and says, "I've got to go, they're waiting." And she just left. And after that, Cleo said, "Well, I'm happy," she said, "I spent one year with my mom and now I can let her go." Yeah, a whole year and then after that she kind of looked up in the ceiling and said, "I have to go. The white horses they came after me. They're waiting."

Part of how Sun Dance got started is because Lupe make a commitment to *hambleceya*. He do that because his mom lived one more year. But, he also *hambleceya* because, years earlier, she had been by his side in the hospital. This was when she was well. The family was all together. It was Easter Sunday. And, Lupe got stabbed. He got stabbed. This was years ago, when Lupe was working for Dale. We were always going to dance—Mexican dance.

LUPE: It was Easter Sunday.

MELDA: It was on Easter Sunday and we had a big Easter dinner with everyone. Lupe wanted to go to the dance. And I said, "Not tonight. We're going to stay home. Because we had a big day." But, he still wanted to go. And, it was kind of late, too. So, I said, "Well, I'll take you." Because I'm always driving. And, at that time, I don't drink. Because I couldn't drink and have fun and all this because I had a lot of kids to take care of. I cannot afford hangovers. I have to get up. So, I said, "Well, I'll drive you if you want to go." So I took him. And when we got to the dance, there was a lot of people. A lot of people.

LUPE: First of all we walked in. I walked to the bar and I got myself a beer. And there was a band playing the mambo. I like to dance. But, I didn't dance because I was waiting for Melda to come back from the bathroom. And, there was man standing right there. I've known him for a lot of years. He's a bad man, you know. Mexican guy. He killed his brother-in-law one time. He was on parole. So I was walking around and he called me a bad name. Back then, I was young and I had a lot of strength in me. I could pick up three hundred pounds over my head. Every Friday and Saturday, I get into fights. Every week. And I never get beat up. I could fight five guys at the same time. I put them away. I don't know how I did it, but I did it. I'm a dirty fighter, you know.

So, this night, there was three guys. And the one in the middle was the one saying bad things to me. He called me outside. I fought all three of them. I beat them up real good and I broke his nose. And I thought it was over, you know. I walk away. And then I feel something in my stomach. Something *hot* in my stomach. He stabbed me in my stomach. Seven inches deep and an inch and a half wide. Inside my stomach. I got the knife and I pull it out. I was strong, you know. I got the knife out. And then I knock him out. Melda was no place in sight. She was still back there. She was having a hard time getting back because there was a lot of people. You could hardly walk. So I was dressed in white, you know, I used to dress real good. Real nice pants, clothes, shoes and all that. And my hair was short. Combed like Elvis Presley all up, and all that. I walk out. And my friends they were scared of me. I was bleeding. Covered in blood. I was all bloody. The bartender—a man and a woman—they know me. This bar they know me pretty good. So I went to a phone and I called my boss and I talked to him. I don't know what I said. And, then I fainted. I pulled the whole phone off. They told me. The ambulance came.

MELDA: I came out from the bathroom and there was nobody there. So I went to the bar and the lady told me, she said, "Lupe got stabbed." And I was thinking, "Oh. Okay, he got stabbed."

LUPE: I was in a coma. For a long time. About a month. I don't know nothing.

MELDA: Back then, Lupe used to be really fat.

LUPE: *Fat.*

MELDA: They say that fat saved him! If he wasn't fat, that knife would have stuck way back in there. So he went through surgery. And, Lupe's mom stayed there all night long with him.

LUPE: Day and night. Day and night.

MELDA: We told her to go home. She said, "No." She stayed with Lupe day and night and there was nobody was going to take her home. Like, me, I could go visit. I had kids I had to go watch so I couldn't stay there. But she stayed there until he was up. And, he remember that she did that.

LUPE: In them days, when I talked about the eagle changing my life, you know, my life was just fighting and drinking. I lived a dangerous life; a wasted life. Every week I get into a fight. Then, I changed my life around good. My whole life turned. I don't fight no more. I pray with my family, my relatives.

MELDA: So, Lupe said, "I'll *hambleceya* for my mom and for all the old people." After Lupe's mom died, we started going with Ruben Fire Thunder to sweat. Lupe was going with Ruben Fire Thunder. Lupe had seen that eagle years earlier. When I took my dad and mom over there to see that eagle, my dad said, "Well, Lupe's going to be a good man." And, then Lupe decide to *hambleceya*. Before he go up the hill, Ruben asked Lupe to go over there for a special ceremony. So they had a ceremony and that's when he adopt Lupe. His brother.

LUPE: My brother.

MELDA: He sweat and he say, "He's going to be my brother because he's been praying this way and he's a strong believer." So he adopt him and we had a nice ceremony and a dinner for him and after that Lupe went to *hambleceya* for four days. He went up the hill.

LUPE: Yeah, he took me up.

MELDA: Lupe said he was going to go up the hill for the elderlies. There were a lot of elderlies there. My aunts . . . a lot of people. My aunt brought three kinds of *wasna*. He came down the hill and it was pretty strong because they support him. Lupe took a blanket up to *hambleceya*. When he came down the hill Ruben told him, he said, "You give that blanket away." Because the way they do it is you pray with that and when you come down you give that blanket to the person who is sick, or been sick. So he taught us in a real good way. At that time Rachel, my sister-in-law, was sick and Lupe gave that blanket to her. She was really happy.

So that's why Lupe went to *hambleceya* because of his mom and for the elderlies. And there was a lot of elderly people there and they really thanked Lupe. They said, "That was really nice, son-in-law. To do this for us." Because in South Dakota, everybody, the older ones, they would call him "son-in-law."

LUPE: Me and Ruben sit in the sweat lodge. Just me and him praying for people. He put a lot of things in my head.

MELDA: Good things.

LUPE: Old man, Ruben. Old guy, you know, big thoughts. It's a good thing—the traditional ways. He told me, one time, he said, "Brother ..." And I listen. He was a funny man sometimes, you know, he really make you laugh. In the ceremonies, talking to him, makes you laugh. So he'd be talking to you real serious and then he'd pop a joke.

MELDA: Really good sense of humor.

LUPE: So, he said, "Brother," and we sit down, we're waiting to go sweat. We're waiting for Uncle Tom. Everything ready. Put the rocks in—me and him. He talked to me. He said, "Brother, what are you doing here?" I joke and I say, "Waiting for Uncle Tom!" I think he might be joking. He said, "Brother, the thing we're doing here is really powerful. Things we have to do. Not for ourselves. For the people. We're going to do this for the people. Not for ourselves."

And he talked to me about a Sun Dance. He said, "I been running this Sun Dance, brother." He said, "The spirits came and told me that we need to move." He said, "We're going to move the Sun Dance down here. Down east." So I went and talked to my mother-in-law the next day and I told Melda about it and we sit down and talk. My mother-in-law agree with it. She was happy.

MELDA: She was happy.

LUPE: We start it and Melda's oldest brother, Albert, was there too, you know.

MELDA: Albert, and Ruben's wife, Pansy, and my mom. My mom, Albert, Pansy, Ruben, Lupe. Those four went looking for a place where they could put up the Sun Dance. Me and Lupe just followed them. Me and Lupe was following them and they found the place and Ruben prayed. I was standing way back.

LUPE: He stop one place and he look around. Look around and then he said, "Brother, let's go that way." Okay. We stop there, he look around again. Right there where we have the arbor. He look around and he and walk again. But, then he look back to that spot. Then he said, "Let's go back." We follow him. Right there where the arbor is, he stood there, facing west. He started singing. Say a prayer when he sings. "Right here, brother. Next year there's going to be a Sun Dance here. A lot of people gonna come. We'll get together."

The way he was telling me, "we'll get together," I didn't get it into my head. He was telling me he was dying. He was dying. He never told me, "I'm dying." He never told me that. He said, "Brother, we're going to build this Sun Dance here." But, he was dying.

It was winter, so we went to work in Arizona. And, one day, I opened a letter. I was reading it and here tears were coming out, you know. The day I got that letter my brother was buried.

When I went back, when I came back to Allen again, I didn't know what to do. So we talk about Sun Dance again. So I talked to Pansy, Uncle Tom, my mother-in-law. Albert was there. We agreed that I was going to build a Sun Dance for four years. In memory of Ruben Fire Thunder and the way he started it. Ruben told me how to build the sweat lodge and the arbor. He told me how to do it.

MELDA: Ruben Fire Thunder was old. When we met him he was like seventy. Yeah, that's *old*. My mom said he used to run around down east with Albert. When Albert was a boy and Ruben was in his twenties. And, he was my cousin. He was half brother of my cousin.

When my mom first hear that he was a medicine man, she was saying, "*Him*? Ruben?!" They say, "I can't believe that he's a medicine man. He used to be really crazy when he was young!" And, one time, we went over for a ceremony. Right near our house down east is Emma Waters's house. And my mom went over there and Ruben was there and she was talking to Ruben and she said, "I didn't know you become a medicine man. *How'd* you do it?!"

So then Lupe had to build the arbor. He had to put up the Sun Dance. But, we was still living in Scottsbluff. So I took Lupe down east and put that tepee up. This was early April. I took some food over there. And, I left him there.

LUPE: Me and my dogs.

MELDA: Beauty and Beast. Real good dogs. One had different kinds of eyes. We went to visit over at Emma's house. And, there, we met Rick Eagle Elk. Medicine man.

LUPE: Real good man. Young man. He said hello to me. And he heard that we were going to build a Sun Dance. Emma told him. I never ask him to help, but he told me, "I want to help you." He stay there with me for eighteen days. I made him work! Early in the morning, I cook breakfast. And dinnertime, I cook eggs.

MELDA: Nothing but eggs.

LUPE: Eggs in the morning, dinner, and supper. I get up early in the morning and we cut logs. In the afternoon we haul them. Just me and him. I work like that until we run out of food. No more eggs!

It was hard. My brother told me that, you know. Ruben told me, he said, "Brother, the Sun Dance is going to be coming and you're going to be there. And it's going to be hard. It's not going to be easy. It's going to be really hard." He told me that. I didn't pay much attention to him. I didn't know what he meant by hard.

MELDA: They were living in a tepee and it took them eighteen days to get all the wood and everything. And the sweat lodge back there. But when they got done, you know, it was really nice. Looks pretty. And, then Lupe wanted to talk to Pansy. He said, "I'm gonna have four years of Sun Dance for my brother. But who's going to run the Sun Dance?" After the arbor was built, we brought Pansy over. And Lupe told them, "We build the arbor now. Everything's done. So who's going to run it?" Pansy said, "Take me to Rosebud. Ruben already told me who's going to run the Sun Dance. We're going to go meet Earl." We found out that when he was dying, Ruben told Pansy, he said, "That Sun Dance we're going to put up down east it's going to be run by Earl Swift Hawk."

So we drove to Rosebud. And that's when I first met Earl and his wife, Edna. They were at a powwow, which was funny. They were at a powwow so we waited outside for them. And they brought him outside and Pansy introduced us to him, "This is Lupe and he build a Sun Dance." So we give him the pipe. He took it for four years. He said, "I'll be over there." We talked to Earl. He said, "That's real good." And he said, "Go ahead and set up the dates and I'll be there."

He said, "I'll run four years for you." That's the first time we met Earl and Edna.

Now it was time for them to set a date. Because this was early spring. So we started that Sun Dance the last part of May to the first part of June. The first week of June. That's how we started. So we came back and we set the dates. And, we had to put drawings on the posters. I had to put the drawings on the poster. I had to come up with that. That first year the Sun Dance poster was really nice. The way I did it, I went to this shop in Scottsbluff and I got some ideas from those T-shirts that have Indian pictures on them. Medicine wheel like this, and then there was a man kind of sitting with the pipe, and the eagle flying with the pipe. I put those three pictures in the middle. But I got this all from T-shirts, all kinds of T-shirts. That's how I did it!

Earl came over there and he start to get ready for the Sun Dance, which was really something for us to experience. And we saw the old people. My mom received the first pipe and pray with it. I stood there and watch her. It was something that I never thought I was going to do.

After my mom died, a few years after we started Sun Dance, I was thinking, "My mom's not going to be around, so why have the Sun Dance?" But she had said, "Melda," she said, "keep the Sun Dance going, because there's a lot of people. A lot of people are going to need that Sun Dance. To come and pray there." She said, "You cannot quit." She said, "What you and Lupe are doing is good. Prayers are strong. Just keep going because it's a good thing. Just keep going. The way these kids are raised now, they're going to learn how to pray the Lakota way. The Sun Dance you'll have here and you could have all your grandkids have name-giving here." You know, she told me that and I said, "Okay." She said, "It's going to be hard, it's going to be really hard. But always remember your prayers." So, when she died, I remembered. I remember what she told me. So that's how Sun Dance got started down here.

8

Generation: Melda

It is by no means a given that those who move toward Lakota tradition later in life are less traditional; and likewise, it is by no means a given that those who have been raised within Lakota tradition necessarily claim an unproblematized identity. All too often there is a failure in the academic community to seriously explore Indian identity as an emerging process, over the course of an individual's life, or to explore dislocation and its effects on Indian identity. Accordingly, Dakota scholar Elizabeth Cook-Lynn cautions against the tendency in the scholarship about the Lakota people "to discuss the divisions on Indian reservations between half-breeds and 'traditionals'" ("How" 88). The political, religious, economic, and cultural suppression of Native cultures has necessarily had an effect on the way individuals are connected to traditional ways. While John Collier legislated against any "interference with Indian religious life or ceremonial expression" in 1934, deterrents continued.[1] Carole Anne Heart Looking Horse (Lakota) says that "[i]t wasn't until 1978, when the American Indian Religious Freedom Act was passed, that our people felt finally they could practice their ceremonies openly in this country" (qtd. in Katz 292). Consequently, as Marjorie Schweitzer explains, "[s]ome [individuals] return[ed] to their native communities and enter[ed] again into Indian social and ceremonial life, learning as retirees what they had missed when they were young" (16).

Melda, who was socialized in a Lakota setting, has been dislocated from the Lakota community to varying degrees and has increasingly moved toward Lakota tradition later in her life. However, these facts do not in any way imply an indistinct connection to what she understands as Lakota tradition. In *Standing in the Light: A Lakota Way of Seeing* (1994), Severt Young Bear (Lakota) describes four circles of people who are present at Sun Dances: those in the center (the dancers), those in the arbor (supporters/singers), those helping around the edge of the arbor, and those who remain further out in the parking lot (Young Bear and Theisz 177). In her life story, Melda similarly describes moving through these circles in her involvement with the Sun Dance. The Sun Dance was restricted by the Bureau of Indian Affairs in the 1880s and was then revived in a public display, associated with an annual fair and organized by the tribal council, in the 1950s and 1960s. Melda recalls going to the sanctioned Sun Dance in 1957:

MELDA: [The Pine Ridge] Sun Dance was in the morning and powwow starts in, like, the afternoon. We always stay there. But, I never did go in the mornings. The old people were there. My mom used to tell us, "You should go there and sit there." And I really regret not having done that. Because, I was like probably sixteen. Probably seventeen. And we sleep late! We always sleep late in the tents. She takes off. Sometimes we get up and we catch the end of it. They do that. I remember Sun Dance, they dance every morning, I don't know why. They didn't dance all day. . . . In those days, nobody really got into these Sun Dances.

In *Bead on an Anthill: A Lakota Childhood* (1998), Delphine Red Shirt (Lakota) describes her experience of the Sun Dance at that time in similar terms:

> Mom-mah and Kah-kah prayed while the carnival rides stopped and started as people purchased tickets for a quarter; the dust at the rodeo flew as the riders with numbers pinned on their backs, dressed in their cowboy boots and brand new jeans, mounted and dismounted with each passing event. The vendors counted change and sold hamburgers, and the dancers danced. The dancers danced in the full sunlight, raising their arms to the sky, sage crowns upon their heads, sage bracelets upon their wrists and ankles. Some carried a hoop made of sage, others a fan made of sage. They danced, ignoring us, as we children ran from one event to the next, spending quarters as fast as we could get them. I was like everyone else there: I ate snow cones and cotton candy. I drank soda pop and ran around the sacred circle. I chased boys and ran to

and from the carnival looking for quarters on the ground. I played
and played, never once stopping, until the last day, to see the faces of
the Sun Dancers . . . [including] the man in the long dark wig. I was
no different from the tourists. I wanted to see what everyone else had
paid to see. (69)

Both accounts attest to the restricted nature of the Sun Dance as
well as the ways in which the younger generation was comparatively
disconnected from Lakota tradition. The older generation supported
the ceremony and encouraged others to learn from the Sun Dance
and move toward the ceremony.

Melda's reconnection with Lakota tradition in the 1970s and 1980s
demonstrates the degree to which identity and tradition are dynamic
processes. Melda asserts that she "grew up in a traditional way," but
she also acknowledges that she "got into this Lakota religion" more
earnestly later in life. She was raised in the Native American Church
and grew up praying with the pipe. She has spoken the Lakota language since childhood. Her family ties to Pine Ridge are extensive.
While I doubt that she would characterize herself as ever being disaf-
fected from Lakota tradition, she has experienced dislocation both
as a migrant worker and while living in urban areas such as Denver,
Colorado, and Scottsbluff, Nebraska. She began, in the 1950s, sleeping
in her tent in the "parking lot" at the BIA Sun Dance. This type of
support is essential to the ceremony. There is a network of people who
work together in supporting the Sun Dance. All of the individuals,
together, enact and propel tradition. James Fenelon says that "[s]ocietal
integrity and group polity . . . grow out of and are essential to the
sundance" (290). Melda's description of her initial estrangement from
aspects of traditional practice, typical for many of her generation,
accords honor to a tradition that both survives and impresses upon
a new generation that they are able to move through the circles that
encompass ceremony. As Dakota scholar Joyzelle Gingway Godfrey
says: "We are here, we are surviving, we are living our traditions,
we do go to sweats, we do have *Wopila* [thanksgiving] ceremonies,

people still sun dance, people still go on vision quests, all of these things we still have . . . [W]e're still there. And we're still strong" (qtd. in Gardner 473).

In tracing her own process of continually moving toward tradition, Melda encourages her children and grandchildren to also move toward tradition. In her story about medicine man Ruben Fire Thunder and his efforts to help Lupe's mother, she talks about tradition as an emerging process. She describes the difficult task of preparing for a *yuwipi* ceremony in Scottsbluff, Nebraska.[2] A young dog is ritualistically cooked for the ceremony as a way of according respect and honor in the Lakota tradition.[3] Referring to her experiences in the ceremony, Melda says: "When I was young I used to go there to ceremony [*yuwipi*], but I've never actually cooked a dog and all these things." Melda emphasizes her role in cooking for the ceremony, and in fact, "[m]uch of the preparation that goes into a feast and give-away is in the hands of females" (Albers, "Sioux" 214). Melda acknowledges that she had to learn how to be involved beyond being a participant; she had to learn about the preparations for the ceremony. Elsewhere she describes how she made *wasna* (pemmican) and *wojapi* (chokecherry pudding), foods that are used ritualistically in ceremonies. In describing her ability to cook *wasna* and her inability to cook a dog, Melda describes herself as both knowing and not knowing about traditional practices. She unsettles the totalizing discourses associated with Lakota tradition and demonstrates her own process of learning about traditional practices. She also highlights the effects of dislocation on Lakota tradition, noting that "[t]here was no way you were going to start a fire outside in Scottsbluff." This highlights the incongruity between a rural traditional past and the contemporary urban situation. Her effort to live a traditional life in an urban locale is what makes her story seem ironic; or, more specifically, her story shows that living in a city makes traditional life seem somehow inconsistent.

At times, Melda and Lupe relate elements of the contemporary urban situation in their daily life experiences. In her life story account, Melda mentions films, namely *The Horse Whisperer* (1998) and, in chapter 9, *The Lion King* (1994). Additionally, Lupe loved to watch Westerns and had extensive knowledge of all the classics. Along these lines, Melda often tells a story about their visit to the Grand Ole Opry. She likes country-and-western music and was especially upset, as a young girl, with the passing of Hank Williams (1923–53). She had always wanted to go to the Grand Ole Opry and, before he died, her son Peto arranged a VIP visit for her. She describes the trip that she took with Lupe, her son, Marcos, and her friend Millie Black Bear to see Skeeter Davis and Garth Brooks:

MELDA: So, I always wanted to go to Grand Ole Opry. That was with everyone in South Dakota—I wish one day I will see Grand Ole Opry 'cause that's where it all started. Country and western. So, I always say, "I wish someday I'll go see Grand Ole Opry." And that year, when we went to visit Peto, he said, "Mom, we're going to take you to Grand Ole Opry." And I said, "What?!" He said, "We're going to take you to Grand Ole Opry." Him and his friends got together . . . and took care of everything. Way in the front they put seats for us. And that was *really* something I'll never forget. "Mom, you always wanted to see Grand Ole Opry," he said, "you're going to see Grand Ole Opry." And he said, "We've got a surprise for you." With Skeeter Davis. She said—I guess he told her to announce us, so she did. She said, "I want to welcome Marcos Red Bear and the Lupe Trejo family who are here from the Great Sioux Nation." They tell us all to stand up and take a bow. That was on TV. So we were on TV. So, my dream came true. I was always telling them I wanted to see Grand Ole Opry. I saw it. And, after that, we went up behind stage, too. We even took a picture with Garth Brooks!

I had often thought that this story was significant because it shows how Indians can have a particular kind of status in "outside" situations. Here, they are recognized as being from the "Great Sioux Nation." However, Melda tells this story quite a lot, and what I found interesting was the way in which the younger members of the family also react to the story. In this particular instance, Melda and Lupe's grandson Pablo (Paul) was present for the recording of the story. He would normally stay quiet, but in this instance, in his preteen years, he interjects: "Yup. They still got the picture with Garth Brooks!" It seems that these types of stories function to communicate in much the same way that they would in any other culture—as a way to find meaning and share particular values and experiences among friends and family. The same can be said of discussions about traditional practices.

In her narrative, Melda shows how her knowledge of Lakota culture reaches back to her great-grandparents. In one of the initial comments in her life story narrative, she says, "I'm the seventh generation from my great-grandfathers." She invokes the Native discourse of "seven generations" as a way of situating herself in the community and demonstrating her responsibility to that community. Dakota scholar Vine Deloria Jr. elaborates on the meaning of "seven generations":

> A good family could anticipate that a child born into it would know and remember his great-grandparents. If that person lived a good life, she would live to see her great-grandchildren. Each person, we might say, is the fourth generation and looks back to three generations and forward to three. When the old chiefs spoke of the seventh generation they were basically saying that they wanted their great-grandsons, whom they hoped one day to see, to have the same rights and privileges as they themselves did. So instead of being a vague term for time, seven generations has a reality and precision within the family context as specific as any written contract ever drawn. (For 179)

Melda conveys the knowledge that she has derived from her parents' generation and her great-grandparents' generation.[4] Herself a great-grandmother, she fulfills her role in maintaining seven generations of Lakota tradition. In this way, she conveys her kinship ties in the Lakota community.

Melda uses ancestry and cultural knowledge to describe Lakota tradition and her position in the community. At one point she mentions uncles who "have different names but they come from the family." She traces her kinship ties and shows how her genealogy extends into both the past and the future.[5] These *tiyospaye*, or smaller kin groups, are significant to the organization of the Lakota community.[6] Cook-Lynn says that the *tiyospaye* "is so much a part of the storytelling process for the Sioux . . . [because it is] a nationalistic forum for the people" (*Why* 93). In her storytelling, Melda recounts the people who were involved in their long path to the Sun Dance. She authorizes her own role in the Lakota community through her associations with specific individuals and practices. She does so, however, in an encompassing manner in that her "[s]tories serve to both establish and legitimate the poles of the dialectic that creates tradition" (Bucko 145). In *The Lakota Ritual of the Sweat Lodge*, Raymond A. Bucko elaborates that stories "not only guide the dialectical process but also become part of the process itself" (145). Accordingly, Melda's stories demonstrate the ways in which Lakota tradition is experienced as a dynamic and regenerative process. She shows how that process is spoken of and talked about. In using kinship ties, Melda is establishing herself within a national discourse, one that upholds the Lakotas as a sovereign nation. Lakota scholar Beatrice Medicine describes *tiyospaye* obligations as a core foundation in Lakota identity.[7] "Our kinship ties, though anachronistic in some instances, bond us together in a Lakota identity," she says (qtd. in Harjo and Bird 209). Melda's Lakota identity is supported through her connections to her relations, and by using this forum she is putting forth knowledge that pertains to the preservation of the Lakota nation.

1. Commemorative photos made for Melda and Lupe's fortieth "wedding" anniversary. Photo courtesy of Melda Trejo.

2. Melda and Lupe at their fortieth-anniversary celebration, Allen, South Dakota, 1998. Photo courtesy of Melda Trejo.

3. Solomon Red Bear, Melda's father (child, *third from left*), Philip Red Bear, Melda's great-grandfather (*front, seated, third from right*), and Charles Red Bear, Melda's grandfather (*back, far right*), ca. 1916. Photo courtesy of Edna Janis.

(*Opposite top*) 4. (*From left*) Melda Red Bear, Berta Crow Dog (sister of Leonard Crow Dog), and Lucille Red Bear (Melda's sister), in Martin, South Dakota, before 1957. Photo courtesy of Melda Trejo.

(*Opposite left*) 5. Melda Red Bear, early 1950s. Photo courtesy of Melda Trejo.

(*Opposite right*) 6. Melda Red Bear, ca. 1960. Photo courtesy of Melda Trejo.

7. Solomon Red Bear, Melda's father (*standing*), and White Star, Melda's cousin (*seated*, *middle*), "down east" in Allen, South Dakota. Photo courtesy of Melda Trejo.

8. Howard Red Bear (paternal great-uncle) "down east" before 1968. Photo courtesy of Melda Trejo.

9. Melda Trejo picking sage "down east."
Photo courtesy of Jimmy and Brenda Trejo.

10. (*From left*) Solomon Red Bear (Melda's father), Henry Crow Dog, and Howard Red Bear (uncle). Photo courtesy of Melda Trejo.

Two Cultures We Have to Put Together

LUPE: You know something . . . Melda's mother could cure the eyes. With a cattail. She'd take a cataract and work on it.

MELDA: She works on people's eyes. My mom.

LUPE: Maybe on cataracts.

MELDA: I've seen her do it. She uses that razor-sharp grass.

LUPE: A grass.

MELDA: It's like razor sharp. And cut the cataracts out.

LUPE: Cut the cataracts out. They know how to do it. I don't know how, but I've seen her do it.

MELDA: It takes her about a week for her to do that. People would say, "I feel good. I can see good." I never did ask how she did it.

LUPE: Not many people know how to do that. Me, I would take the whole eye out!

MELDA: She used to do that, my mom.

LUPE: Way before doctors. They do it before doctors.

MELDA: They use that laser now or something.

LUPE: My mother, too. My mother cure people, too. A different way, though. Her way is with a broom and two eggs and you go out there and pray over the body. When you get in a car accident and you're scared all the time and can't sleep, she'll go out there and clear it up. You'll be all right. A broom.

MELDA: A broom and an egg. The way I see her, she gets the broom first. Puts the person down and she clears and she works all over the body, just like sweeping the body with the broom.

LUPE: All over the body.

MELDA: And then she takes this egg and then she goes and puts it all over the body and she prays and then she breaks that egg and she puts it in the cup. And she takes that broom. And she makes three little crosses and she put it on top of the egg when she breaks it and then she leaves the egg there. And she leaves it overnight. And then you get that egg in the morning and that egg is all no good. It's cloudy. It's no good. And then that person feels well. All that what's inside of her, that's making her hurt and scared, she takes all that out. They go into the egg and the crosses.

LUPE: She learned this from her aunt. Her aunt. A long time back. When she was a young girl. She used that for many people. From Texas to Nebraska and Colorado. In the hospital, too. One time, my cousin got into a big accident and the doctors couldn't help him and he hollers and hollers. My mother got her broom and my cousin was lying down with two nurses and a doctor there. The doctor seen my mother with a broom and they call my mother back: "No, no, no!" They thought she was going to beat him up with it. They don't know. I explain to the doctor that she's going to "doctor." They let her do it. She's got that broom. Sweep everything on his body. From head to toes. The egg. She rub that body all over. Crack that egg. With the broom. Make the crosses and crack that egg. The next day, no more hollering. They let him out of the hospital. She did it. Many times I seen her do that.

My mom believes this way. People thought she was a crazy woman. When lightning comes really hard, she gets a knife, really sharp, in front of that cross and she cries and prays. In front of lightning. And you know what happened? Everything breaks up. The thunder and everything goes away. She believe in these things, you know.

MELDA: Lupe's mom also help women to have the baby. When a woman is going to have a baby and that birth is going to be a breech birth. She fix them up. So they don't have to go have cesarean. I seen her do that. The woman was really sick. She couldn't have her baby because it was going to be a breech birth. Doctors said she was going to have to have a cesarean. His mom goes over there and says, "No, no, no. I'll fix her up." And she did. I don't know how she did it, but she went in there and she couldn't deliver for two days. She went in there and did something to her and the baby turn and got on the right track so they didn't have to operate. So she does that. I seen her. The doctor said, "Hey, what did you do to her?" But she don't speak English so she can't tell him how. She did a lot of good things.

LUPE: People are amazed. But there are people who can do things like that. Each person's got a gift, you know. Each and every one of us has got a gift. But, sometimes we don't use it. We don't. But, we have that gift, each and every one of us.

MELDA: You know, we have seven rites as Indian people. One is the Sun Dance. And one is name-giving. Name-giving ceremony. We have to raise our kids with that eagle feather. When they are small, you have to give them Indian names. I think, when you do the name-giving and you put the eagle feather on, that's their baptismal. That's like the Bible—when you baptize them. So, you see, Indians really don't need that baptizing.

There's something similar to the name-giving in that movie. That cartoon about the lion. *The Lion King.* It reminds me of that because they hold the lion cub up there and pray. Something like that. When they used to do name-giving it was like that. Because they were all ... nothing on ... no clothes on. When the baby was born they paint with red paint, *wasa*, right here in the part in the hair. And they stand outside and pray with them. My great-great-grandmother do that. With my cousin. That was the last time that my uncle saw that. To pray with them like that. That was done like that when they were first born. They say your name and you pray with them. But, there was no clothes on or nothing. And later on they put that eagle feather which is baptismal for the Indian people.

Lupe's culture—Mexican—and mine. We put them together. We do the eagle feather and the name-giving. And, Lupe's culture, when a girl turned fifteen they have this big ceremony for her. *Quincinara.* When you turn fifteen, turn to woman, womanhood, it's just like something like the Indian people do. We had that for our grand-daughter, Rae-Anne. She had her Indian name when, I guess, she was nine years old. And then when she turned fifteen we had her *quincinara*. So we had to do both of them. It was hard for us because we have two cultures. Two cultures is hard. One is hard! We've got to go through two. Try to do both of them. But Mexican way was kind of expensive! Because, you know, they have a white dress. A nice white dress. And, just about everything that she uses she had to have that. A Bible. A cup. Her shoes. Her ring. And a necklace. Earrings. The knife. The dress. The Bible. The crown. And a cake. I think I counted about twelve of them. And, she has to have fifteen godmothers. She had to have fifteen godfathers and fifteen godmothers. Because she's fifteen. And then they have to have fifteen girls which are fourteen years old and under. And fifteen boys. And then this is like a wedding, you know. She wears a white dress. So we did that for her. We saved for like two or three years! We were saving and saving. We saved and we got her dress. It's a white dress and it's especially made for the *quincinara*. And it's got pearls hanging all over, every stitch. It's real beautiful.

And all the Indian people wanted to see that. Because we're always having name-giving. So they wanted to see the Mexican *quincinara*. We had that. And then after that there's a big feast and a dance. Mexican dance. With a band. We had fun. We danced. My cousins. And all these old people. They danced! They really enjoyed it. That was something they'd never been through and, oh, they really enjoyed it. You know, it was real fun. So two cultures we have to put together. So that was really nice.

Through this Sun Dance, I've met a lot of nice people. My dad always teach us to pray with everybody. He said, "That's the only way you're going to see *wichózanni*, good health. It's the only way you're going to go to heaven." He said, "Because God didn't make just Indians. God make all kinds. So if God only wants Indian people to go to heaven, he would have created only Indian people." I believe in what he tells me. You see all kinds of nationalities. And a lot of different kinds. Different kinds of Indians.

Ruben Fire Thunder, too, tells a lot of good things to Lupe. He told him: "Don't put people aside. Welcome everybody." He said, "Because we're all humans." He said, "We're not God to decide who comes in. That's for *Tunkashila* to do that. We're only humans. We're only humans and we were created equal. All humans are created equal and we're not supposed say, "White people, black people: No, you can't come in." Because they're humans and we help each other out. So that's the way he told Lupe.

LUPE: Ruben Fire Thunder told me, he said, "When people come to the arbor, regardless of their color or race, let them in. Don't turn your back on nobody." And I would say it's good to get together with one another regardless of color or race, to get together, and pray. *Tunkashila* and *Wakan Tanka* meant for us to be all together as one. The world was made this way. There's myself. Look at the color I am. Look at yourself. Look at others. But people don't understand that. They look only for certain people; the way people look.

MELDA: We're all Indians, I guess. Just like me I'm not a full-blooded Indian. I'm all different. My mom's a northern Cheyenne. And my great-grandma's a Mexican. My dad's part Mexican and part Indian. So I don't consider myself full-blood. In our area, the Plenty Arrows are maybe full-blooded.

And, we have grandkids all over. In New Mexico we have some. I have twenty-nine grandkids and one great-grandkid. I've got a whole bunch. Twenty-nine grandkids and one great-granddaughter. And I have a Navajo daughter-in-law. I have a Navajo daughter-in-law and I have three of my daughter-in-laws are white. Three of them. Well, Brenda's a different tribe so she's not all white. Raymond is married to an Indian girl, Levina. Levina is my niece. But not too close. Not too close. They're from Martin. On the other side of Martin. I know Levina's mom and I know Levina's oldest brother and sister. They used to come to peyote meeting.

So we have lots and lots of cousins. That's why I told my sons to check with me. When we move back to South Dakota and a girl comes to them and they say, "She came to me and she likes me and all that." And I say, "No, because we're all related." So, they kind of said, "Mom, do you know this . . ." You know, they mention a girl. And I say, "Yeah. They're related to us." And they kind of got tired of that, so they went away and got married to—most of them—white women.

We have a lot of relatives. The whole reservation is our relatives. That's because my great-grandfather had a lot of wives. We come from a big family from the beginning. And I have a lot of aunts, too. And I have a whole bunch of cousins. From my mom's side and my dad's side. Too many! Too many cousins.

So I was sitting there thinking and I said, "How come you boys don't marry to Indian women?" They said, "Mom, you told us we're all related to the Sioux here. You can't marry them!" And I say, "Oh, that's right. Well . . . that's okay then."

LUPE: One time, we talk to Melda's uncle. He was a good man, a respectable man. He's an Indian. Lakota. He said, "You know, it was a long time ago that the Lakota people went to the south and they met the Aztecs over there coming this way. And they met each other over there. And they got together and they adopted each other. They were all Indians." He said, "It doesn't matter if you're white with blue eyes, we've got this blood. And just one drop of blood, you consider yourself an Indian. We're all Indian." He said, "Some people have a hard time believing that. Some of them look at you and criticize you."

So I've told that to many people, what he told us. And he was right, you know. A long time ago that happened. In Mexico, to this day, they've got a pipe. *Chanupa.* And they pray with that. They have traditional prayers. Pray as Aztecs. All day long, praying like that. It's connected, the Lakota people are connected a long time ago, they pray. They pray with rocks and fire, the same as they do over here. Same thing like a Sun Dance. And they use feathers too, but the feathers come from different kind of a bird. Over here, the Lakota people use the eagle and the hawk. That's what they use.

And I've got a lot of aunts, uncles. Right there in the village, Silao. So my father's family is a really traditional people. And they used to play like a football and basketball. Way back. They played those games. They challenge each other, you know. Village to village.

And my father, until the day he died, he was an Aztec. He believe in that way. My father was the only boy in the family. Many sisters. They were all over seven feet tall. Real tall. They're tall ladies. My father was the only short one in the family. And my father's taller than me! My grandfather came from Mexico and left my father when he was nine years old. In Scottsbluff. Somehow, some way he grew up by himself. In Scottsbluff. He turned into a man by himself. So my grandfather he never see him again. My aunts weren't in the United States. He never see them. My father didn't go back to see his family for forty-two years. The Aztecs.

MELDA: And, then, one year, we decided to take Lupe's father back to Old Mexico. That's the first time I went. We took him. That was interesting. In Mexico. So I ask Lupe. Well, in that year the gas was not too high. It was cheap. So, I said, "Let's save some money and take your dad and mom back to Mexico." So I ask him and he said, "Yeah. That would be nice." I wanted to see Mexico City, but we only went to the place where Lupe's father was born. So we stopped there. And he had all his relations there.

LUPE: It's not a small village. It's a pretty good size. It was nice. People would sit and eat outside. Like, I tell Melda, "Look how beautiful." The houses over there are adobe houses.

MELDA: Each of them had their place. It's fenced in and you have your house and then you have your water. And on that you have cows, pigs, chickens.

LUPE: They grow their own things.

MELDA: They eat from there. They didn't go to town.

LUPE: Like one family gets their own milk. Sell their bread. The money stays around. And, when tourists come, they keep all their money and share everything. They sell things at the mall. The *mercado*. They sell machetes.

MELDA: On certain days.

LUPE: Everyone puts up their own stand.

MELDA: They make dresses, clothing. This old man always take milk around.

LUPE: And eggs.

MELDA: Milk and eggs.

LUPE: Where my father lived, they still live in traditional ways. They got houses. And dirt floors. They sleep on the ground. On a rug. They roll it up. Roll it out and go to bed. And young girls, young ladies, they are fifteen- and sixteen-year-olds. They get together and cook for all of us. They're not smoking somewhere and all that, they're right beside us. We're eating and they're watching you eat. See you finished your tortilla and they make one real quick and they give it to you. Ain't it, Melda? They do that. Fresh food, too. They see that you're finished with that one and they've got the other one coming right there.

MELDA: They don't buy flour. They have a lot of corn, they do their own flour right away.

LUPE: Cornmeal. From the corn. They've got a bag, they grind it up. They do that every day.

MELDA: They do that every day. They don't buy flour like we do.

LUPE: They don't go out there and buy the bread or nothing. They just make their own right away. Perfectly round. Fast!

MELDA: They don't use no rolling pin.

LUPE: It's real nice. And they have the watermelon. Big. Each of them has something to sell. And the money stays around. Like a circle. It doesn't go out.

MELDA: We see his aunts. One of the aunts had moved to Mexico City. The youngest. She came from Mexico City. With her son.

LUPE: My nephew over there has got a yacht. He's got a yacht over there to take tourists to the sea. That's his work.

MELDA: She came from Mexico City. She came and she cried.

LUPE: Oh. She was happy. Really happy.

MELDA: She was crying. To see her brother forty-two years later. When the sister came, she was crying and they were talking and talking and she said, "How come you left us?" She told her brother, "We really suffered. We were womens living here. We suffered." They had hard times. So she had to move to Mexico City. They had a really hard time. Waiting for their dad and their brother to come from the United States.

LUPE: Just my father went back. My aunt wanted to come back with us and see the Sun Dance.

MELDA: And, it was really nice. I got to see Old Mexico.

10

Identity

Indian identity itself is lineal and cultural, political and spiritual. However, these structures are interpreted differently according to colonial and traditional viewpoints. Mainstream efforts to define and delimit identity and tradition are subverted by strategic indigenous discourses as well as traditional Lakota perspectives. Prayer, ceremony, and storytelling actively regenerate Lakota tradition, developing a sense of relatedness that extends beyond colonial categorization. This voicing of relations, the claiming of a set of experiences or lineal affiliations, can be seen to sustain Indian identity in contemporary circumstances. At the same time, "[q]uestions of who is a 'real indigenous' person, what counts as a 'real indigenous leader,' which person displays 'real cultural values' and the criteria used to assess the characteristics of authenticity . . . are designed to fragment and marginalize" (Tuhiwai Smith 72). Responses to these pressures are necessarily expected both inside and outside Native communities. Hence, we can see the ways in which indigenous people caught between two worlds are sometimes compelled to "use both kinds of language to claim a legitimate voice" (Cruikshank xv).

In discussing intermarriage specifically, Melda both addresses and discounts racial issues, thereby using both traditional and colonial discourses in her commentary. In particular, she reflects on how most of her sons "got married to white women." That said, those who have married into the Trejo family have supported a commitment to traditional Lakota practices. Of course, matters of the heart are even more significant and complex than those involving ethnicity, but I am here simply focusing on the political aspects of intermarriage. According to Winona Stevenson (Cree), everything becomes political in Native communities, and "the most pervasive politics are personal and familial" (7). In her narrative, Melda recounts the intertribal and cross-cultural marriages of her sons: "Twenty-nine grandkids and one great-granddaughter. . . . I have a Navajo daughter-in-law and I have three of my daughter-in-laws are white. Three of them. . . . Raymond is married to an Indian girl, Levina."

Melda delineates between being mixed-blood, or from another Indian nation, and being Lakota, which in this case is taken to mean "Indian." She has told her children to avoid marrying those to whom they might be related on the reservation, but she implies that she would prefer to have Lakota in-laws by saying, "Well . . . that's okay then." She actually laughs when she makes the comment, and Melda speaks lightheartedly to underscore the irony of her own predicament as a Lakota/Cheyenne/Mexican woman who has married a Mexican man. Melda also further highlights the irony in considering racial issues from a traditional perspective; she is ultimately saying that "it is okay"—that it is not an issue, or rather, that it is a *colonial* issue.

Historically, adoption and intermarriage were traditional practices for the Lakota people and functioned as an expression of the Lakota understanding of relatedness. Adoption often proceeds from the *hunka*, or brother, ceremony and those who are adopted "are also considered in certain contexts insiders, whether they are whites or Lakotas or members of other tribes" (Bucko 221).[1] In "Iyeska Win: Intermarriage and Ethnicity among the Lakota in the Nineteenth and Twentieth Centuries" (1994), LaVera Rose (Lakota) says that "[i]nitially Lakotas embraced outsiders through adoptions, making them relatives with all the comforts and rights of kinship" (13). Alliances were forged, and continue to be supported, through intermarriage, adoption, spiritual relationships, or economic relationships. Rose further claims that "[w]hile Lakotas [traditionally] view ethnicity solely in terms of behavior, Euroamericans base their ethnic membership primarily on race" (100). Allies reinforce the Lakota nation. Relations, therefore, extend beyond categorizations associated with blood quantum. These fluid categories were eclipsed by more rigid and combative ones; the Lakotas increasingly distinguished between allies and adversaries with the institution of the Allotment Act and the claiming of treaty rights.

When discussing intermarriage, Melda invokes traditional outmarriage practices and highlights her position, and that of her family, in the Lakota community.[2] She says, "I have a whole bunch of cousins. From my mom's side and my dad's side. Too many! Too many cousins." She indicates that her sons have not married within the Lakota community because "we're all related to the Sioux here." Melda chooses to disregard urban dislocation or class issues and other factors that might be related to intermarriage. The discussion is framed by her reference to traditional practices and community identity; she stresses her genealogical position in the Lakota community as necessitating outmarriage. During my first to South Dakota, in 1995, I experienced the practice of tracing one's relations in the community. The Trejo family held a large Easter-egg hunt for their immediate family and distant cousins. At the end of the day, the sides of the family lined up facing each other and were introduced to one another with specific mention of familial relation. I was told that the gathering of the relatives functioned to prevent relatives from marrying, and I have since recognized that this practice, as well as what it represents, is important in the construction of Lakota identity. In *Bead on an Anthill: A Lakota Childhood* (1998), Lakota writer and educator Delphine Red Shirt describes traditional outmarriage practices: "'*Witcotakuye hena slolkiya ye*,' she tells me. 'Know who your relatives are' . . . because it was considered taboo to marry a relative, no matter how distant. These were the things she wanted me to know" (96). In her discussions of intermarriage, Melda shows herself as being Lakota in that she is closely related to members of the community, and she thereby indicates that her own choice to marry outside the Lakota community supports traditional cultural practices.

As we have seen, Melda inscribes herself into the Lakota community primarily through family associations. Lupe's emphasis on spiritual ties highlights the different ways Melda and Lupe talk about their relationships with, in this case, the medicine men in the Lakota

community. For example, Melda recounts growing up in close association with the Crow Dog family, and her stories focus on their
formative years. Alternatively, Lupe emphasizes Leonard Crow Dog's
spiritual status and recalls their involvement together in Sun Dances.
In his story about deciding to Sun Dance, Lupe says, "[w]e went up
to medicine man Leonard Crow Dog. He was real young. We were
young." He invokes his association to Leonard Crow Dog and also
highlights that the whole community was "real young," which implies
that he was a *part* of the revitalization of the Indian community.
Lupe is critically aware of his position as an "outsider" in the Lakota
community.[3] Interestingly, from my perspective as an outsider, he
has lived as an insider. Kathleen Pickering asserts that "appeals [are
made] to kinship, adoption, Lakota mentors, personal visions and
dreams and historical documents . . . to establish . . . individual authority" ("Review" 186). The ways in which Lupe aligns with Lakota
mentors, in addition to his mention of visions, serve to bridge his
relations in the community. For instance, in another story Lupe relates
his experiences with Stanley Looking Horse, who acted as keeper of
the sacred pipe of the Lakota people.[4] Stanley Looking Horse has
since died, but he was well known in both Native and non-Native
communities. Once again, Melda speaks elsewhere of her family's
historical association to the pipe while Lupe emphasizes spiritual
strength. Lupe indicates how Looking Horse supported his prayers in
the sweat lodge. Additionally, before Lupe's first *hambleceya*, Ruben
Fire Thunder adopted Lupe, in the Lakota tradition, as his brother.
Melda mentions her mother's memories of Ruben Fire Thunder as
a young boy, but she also emphasizes the spiritual and cultural ties
between her husband and Ruben Fire Thunder. Melda talks primarily about family relationships, childhood experiences, and people of
previous generations; Lupe maintains a distinct connection to the
Lakota community in his appeals to spiritual authorities.

Lupe posits his identity as an Aztec who supports Lakota spiritual
practices in terms that are transhistorical and cross-continental. He
acknowledges that he is from a "different tribe" but nonetheless iden-

tifies as an Indian, reconfiguring ethnicity in ways that challenge the fragmentation associated with colonization. He characterizes a historical pattern of intermarriage as being a traditional Indian practice. He asserts that Indians across the North American continent—in this case, understandably, the Lakotas and Aztecs—met up with each other and intermarried. Other ethnic groups invariably become implicated in this cross-cultural practice of intermarriage, and therefore he regards everyone as being Indian: "You know, it was a long time ago that the Lakota people went to the south and they met the Aztecs over there coming this way. And they met each other over there. And they got together and they adopted each other. They were all Indians. . . . In this day, we're all mixed. . . . And just one drop of blood, you consider yourself an Indian. We're all Indian."

Lupe structures his understanding of Mexican identity using a narrative that undercuts the colonial apportionment of the North American continent and peoples.[5] He regards himself in relation to a composite mythology that displaces colonial and tribal understandings of racial divisions; he rewrites blood-quantum criteria by stressing that "one drop" of Indian blood dictates Indian identity.[6] His multiple negotiations of Indian identity make a powerful statement about the way in which he conceives of race and, more importantly, about the way in which he conceives of the colonial construction of race and ethnicity. Race matters, but not in the way we thought it mattered.

Racial criteria have come to be associated with Indianness through the implementation of government policies and the absorption of dominant ideologies.[7] Ideas about truth and authenticity have been taken up in Native communities and have influenced what it means to be Lakota. Correspondingly, intermarriage is an issue in the lives of Melda and Lupe, as it is for many other contemporary Indians. Tribal and reservation systems, which began as bureaucratic tools to subsume diverse peoples under a single classification, have contributed to present-day identities that have "resulted from the interaction between governmental policies and indigenous responses to them" (Kurkiala 137). In their life stories, Melda and Lupe respond to, resist, and overwrite conventional understandings of Indian identity. According to Leroy Little Bear (Blood), this is part of "what it means to be colonized" (85). Maori critic Tuhiwai Smith elaborates: "it means that there is unfinished business, that we are still being colonized (and know it), and that we are still searching for justice" (34). Indigenous communities respond by revisiting history because "race" and other characteristics denoting ethnic affiliation remain contested. At the same time, local knowledge emerges from cultural traditions that existed long before there was an empire to which a response could be offered. Native communities are not just "writing back" or "talking back" (see King). In this case the Lakota tradition contributes theories about the world that we seem to understand only from a postcolonial position, but these theories tell us something very new about that position, namely, that it is not the only one.

PART III

Tradition

11

I Spend My Life in Church

MELDA: When we moved back to South Dakota, we went to Ruben Fire Thunder's a lot. And he adopted Lupe as a brother. We had eighteen ceremonies in a row. We had sweats. And after that he tell Lupe lots, you know.

When we go into ceremony at that time, they talk in real Lakota language. And, I can't understand. They don't talk like we do now. Everyday language. But when they talk with "jawbreakers" words, it's really hard to understand. Because we don't talk like that. But those old people do. Especially when we go in ceremonies, they use those words. And I say, "What do you mean? What's he saying?" But, I have my mom there and she always tell me. She knows. She always tell me what they mean. And, I say, "Oh." I said, "But now, you know, we say it different." She said, "That's the Lakota language." And, so, with my cousins, we talk Lakota language. But if an old man comes or an old woman comes, that's different. They use real hard words. So I guess we have two language. Two—one is hard and one's easy to understand.

When Sun Dances started up in the 1970s and '80s, we first went to Crow Dog's. There was also Fire Thunder and Vernal Cross. That's it, that I remember. That's about it. I think John Around Him start after ours.

LUPE: After we started ours, a lot of people started to do them. Right on the reservation right now, there's so many Sun Dance, I don't know how many there are, but there's *lots*.

MELDA: You know, Sun Dancing didn't really get started until AIM people. In 1973. Wounded Knee and after that. Sun Dances started.

And, in the 1980s, they tried to start up the Ghost Dance. Yeah. The Ghost Dance. Sarah Thunder Hawk's son, John, start that in

Porcupine. He had a dream that he was supposed to do Ghost Dance. So he did. They danced. And we support them.

LUPE: We went over there. There were eight of us. And, they were looking for whoever danced the Ghost Dance to shut it down. It's not allowed. Ghost Dance is really powerful. Really powerful.

MELDA: It used to be *really* powerful. But white people stopped that. A long time ago, they had the Ghost Dance. My mom talked about this old lady in a Ghost Dance. She falls down and she goes into the other world. In the other world, they tell her something. Or she brings something back. I heard her talk about that. When she falls they're not supposed to pick her up or anything. Leave her alone. So she goes into the other world. One time she brought back *wasna. Wasna.* And she's supposed to feed all the people. That was the medicine. It was good because they could have one day brought back medicine that could cure cancer. That's my thinking. She also brought back *wasa,* that sacred red paint. Those two things she brought back. And that was when the *wasicus,* the white man, say they're not supposed to be having the Ghost Dance. Because, I don't know, they were scared, I guess. They got scared.

LUPE: They were scared.

MELDA: They try to make it illegal.

LUPE: Thought it was bad medicine, I guess.

MELDA: So that would be something powerful.

LUPE: Strong.

MELDA: Strong. Really strong. But, that Ghost Dance in Porcupine, he just had it one year. And he just didn't have it anymore. He tried to bring it back, but I guess it was not meant for people to bring that back. So nobody did. So they got into Sun Dancing.

They did have the Sun Dance. Before. At the powwow in 1955. When I was growing up, I used to go to powwow. Over there in Pine Ridge. And, they had that Sun Dance over there. I watched Sun Dance in 1955, 1956, 1957. But, it's just four mens dancing for one day. Sun Dance was only like for the old men. There was not a lot of people involved, then. It was just one day. Four old men dancing, and then they pierced. There were only four of them. Yeah. And I watched that because I used to be a traditional dancer, powwow dancer. In 1955. I used to dance. Powwow dance. The whole family used to dance. I'm really glad that I danced with my aunts. And my uncles. My dad never did dance. He was a minister. Peyote. He always support us though.

I wasn't interested in dancing, but my mom put me out there with the beaded dress. My mother says, "You gotta do this." Me and my friends and she entered us in there. It was a beautiful dress that my grandmother loaned to me. When she brought that it was all beaded. The whole thing was beaded. But, I didn't want to use the moccasins. I was kind of bashful: "I'm not going to go out there." So my aunts came over and they were helping me get ready. There were a lot of old people there from Pine Ridge. A lot of old people. I remember my uncle saying, he told me, he says, "Daughter, you gotta do this because your mom wants you to." I said, "Okay. Okay, I'll go." In those days, we have to listen!

That was the last year that I dance, because my sister got killed in a car accident in Pine Ridge. So I just never went back to dancing. I just sort of quit. That's when I met Lupe and I didn't go back. But, we went to Pine Ridge to that dance in 1957.

We used to go to a lot of powwows. My mom. My dad didn't. He just takes us, he didn't go to a lot of powwows. But in those powwows they never have those jingle dress. It was just, like, traditional. I never did see jingle dress, or fancy, or shawl. I guess that started later. So we used to go to powwow. All of us. And we used to make our own costumes. A buckskin dress and moccasins. My mom did all that. My brothers, Norman and Junior, they used to do their own costumes.

My sister-in-law, Lupe's sister, met Norman at the powwow. Cleo really liked him because he was a dancer. She said, "I really like your brother and his feathers." She says, "I want to meet your brother." And I took her to powwow with me the first time. Because she wanted to go with me. And she started talking to Norman. About a year later, they eloped together. They got married in Church of God. It's a missionary church.

Church of God was a Lakota missionary church that came to Scottsbluff and everybody was going there. Mr. and Mrs. Bailey came to Scottsbluff in 1955. And when they came to Scottsbluff, they didn't have no church, so we just set that up. The Indian missionaries borrow a church. And years later, they start building their own church. They build a house first. And in that house, in the basement was the church that we used to go to. And then he started building the church beside the house. So we went there. We used to go with our parents to church.

I was helping with the church for a long time. I grew up there. You know, teenage years I always go to that church and help out and help them cook. And we helped her can. You know, do a lot of things. My granddaughter asked me one time, "Grandma, what did you do when you was young?" I said, "You know, I grew up in Mr. and Mrs. Bailey's church. Because that's where we had fun." I said, "I grew up in church most of the time because there were no TVs and all this. I spend my life in church."

Later on, Mr. and Mrs. Bailey left Nebraska. They got old. That church—you hardly see any Indian people there. Nobody goes there. But, in our days, that church was going pretty good. And I was kind of sad when they left. But she comes back now and then. She's real nice.

I learned a lot of family values in church. The things you have to do. It did me some good, you know. So maybe that's one of the reasons I didn't want to get married in Catholic church because I was mostly going to Church of God. And I used to go there with Lupe. I took my kids to Mr. and Mrs. Bailey's church. My other brother, Junior, got married there. I don't know why they never got married in Native American Church.

My dad was minister in Native American Church, but when we moved to Scottsbluff most of the time we go to Church of God. But they still have their Native American Church meetings. So I grew up going to those meetings, too. Until I was sixteen years old. In 1957, when my sister got killed, I stopped going to peyote meetings. The pipe was always there, though. And I grew up in ceremonies. My mom used to go to ceremonies a lot. *Yuwipi* ceremony.

My dad was a Catholic a long time ago when they got the land down east. They were all Catholics because there was only that Catholic priest who was down there. Going all around there, down east, on a horse. He was going around telling all these Indian people that they should be baptized because, he said, "If you're not baptized, you're going to go to hell." You know, so they all believed him! They didn't want to go to hell. They all got baptized in Catholic church. So, all my grandfathers, they were all baptized as Catholics. Because of what they told them. The *wasicus* came and told them they're going to go to hell if they're not baptized. And, it's funny, then we have to get baptized. If we don't, if we're not baptized, we're all gonna go to hell. So . . . well, I don't want to go to hell, do I?

My father was a minister in the Native American Church. My brother, Junior, was a minister in the Native American Church. The Native American Church started in South Dakota in 1914. Three men came from Oklahoma City. They were Cheyenne. They came to South Dakota and they introduced the peyote. And then the first meeting they had was down east. It started from down east. It was my grandfather, my great-grandfather, who started it in South Dakota. Philip Red Bear. Runs Along the Edge Red Bear. He was the first one. And two other men. My uncle, Ed Richards. And Jim Blue Bird. He's buried up here. They introduced peyote to the Lakota people. In 1914.

So they had peyote meetings and they sing songs. And, I guess, it was going pretty strong. So they took up that religion—the peyote. Back then, it wasn't the Native American Church. It was just peyote. It wasn't called Native American Church. And, back in those days it was . . . illegal. They wanted to put them in jail. So they have to . . . you know . . . crawl underground. They have to hide. They just tell a few people who goes to that meeting. They have the meetings way back in there. Don't tell a lot of people where they have it. Because

Pine Ridge was really coming on strong. They wanted to catch them. And they did catch them! They got caught with the peyote. And my great-grandfather, Philip Red Bear, went to jail. Yeah. They took him to Deadwood! They put him in jail over there. Deadwood.

Philip had to get a lawyer. So he got a lawyer from Martin. And he had to put up a section of land. He put up the land for the lawyer to get him out of that mess. It's a farm land, too. It's going towards Martin. See, all this land . . . Runs Along the Edge, when they settled there, he was really smart because he had all his sons living in tents clear over to the road. He had all that land. Whole bunch of acres going from the house way over to Highway 18. Many people have sold that. But, he was pretty smart, you know. Taking all that land going towards Martin.

They got legal records because of his arrest. This is how we know a lot about how the peyote came to South Dakota. Because Pine Ridge has got records. And the records say that Philip lost pretty good land. When he got out of jail, they fought for peyote. They made it legal. And then they call it Native American Church. And they were pretty strong. And they used the pipe, too. What I heard: they go into sweat and they come out and they go to the meeting with the pipe. Philip Red Bear used both of them—pipe and peyote. He did it real good, you know. He was real strong. So it started from Allen. A lot of people don't know this. But that's where it started from.

So later on, when they passed away, my dad was still going strong. And I used to go to that church. I used to sit in there. Until I was sixteen years old. I used to go with my dad every Saturday night. Yeah. Me and my sister used to sit in there. But what he did was he never gave us . . . we never ate peyote. It was the juice. He always said, "Drink a little bit, you know, and just stay in here." So we did that. I never experienced that peyote, you know, when you take a whole bunch. Never. He knew you're not supposed to. He didn't play with it. He just give us a little bit.

They used to have meetings in Scottsbluff when we lived over there. And on Sundays, they used to go to dinners. And, Lupe's dad was visiting with us. And he says, "The Aztecs used that peyote." And Lupe's dad start telling stories about where it comes from. He said, "It used to grow in the ocean. Bottom of the ocean." Now, that was interesting. He said the ocean was way up covering the land. The water. A long time ago. Old Mexico used to be in an old ocean. And the peyote was in the ocean. I said, "I didn't know that." And I told my mom and she was really interested. And she said, "Really? I didn't know that." It comes from the Aztec. But they didn't drink it or eat it, they used it in a different way. They use it for healing. They put it on if you have sores, they put it on their skin like a poultice. Aztec ways. So it's a traditional way for the Aztecs; not for the Lakota people. I don't think it's connected with traditional ways. It came to South Dakota in 1914. So it didn't go way, way back like people say. Peyote is not traditional, because they brought that from Cheyenne. It did go way, way back for the Aztecs. And, later it came to South Dakota. And, it start from down east.

Philip lost land to come out of jail for that peyote. Land is a real big issue. And, right now, they're talking about taking the Black Hills back. They're on to that again. Here's my thinking: just let it go. Because we're never going to live on that land. And, what we need is land to live on. They've already got everything out of the Black Hills. So they should just get the money. And we can help ourselves. What we have to have are small lands. Not lease it out. What I look at in South Dakota, the biggest problem is land. I don't care about the other ones. I think our biggest problem is the land. We have to do something so we can take our land back. To live on.

We want to put a buffalo, maybe one or two, on that land. Next year, I'm trying to get chickens and a pig. And we're trying to buy a buffalo. I think Pine Ridge will loan you the male and you can breed them. And then you get your buffalo going that way.

They lease the land out. They lease the Indian people's land. And, they have cows on that leased land. They turn them lose and they just let them go. That's their responsibility, not ours. The cows won't keep away from the cemetery down east. It's a Native American Church cemetery. It was donated to my grandfather when he was living. In other words, it's from our family and we have to take care of it. I'd like to fix it up. Secure it good so the cows won't go in there. They destroy all those headstones. One is cracked because they knock it down. I'm going to say that people spend a lot of money for those headstones. And I did too—on my mom and my sister, Lucille, and my dad. It cost a lot of money. And then those cows go in there.

I'm going to put up a meeting, a land meeting, and bring all that up. Bring all that up. I'm going to write everything down and have a meeting. One time they had a meeting and I went over there and I called everybody that was concerned. And, you know what? They didn't show up! I was the only one talking. I said, "Oh, this is bad. I've got to call for backup."

When we have meetings, often people are just arguing. My mother told me, "You don't open your mouth if you're going to say something bad. If you're going to say something good, then you open your mouth. Let something good come out. But if you're going to open your mouth and hurt people, don't open your mouth." Yeah, so, you know, I always remember. Sometimes, it's better to just sit there and listen. So I learned a lot from my mom. Because sometimes I catch myself when I want to say something and instead I start thinking before I say anything.

I try to do real good. I try to help around here where I live. Pass Creek district. I helped cook for this memorial dinner. Yeah. That was really good. That lady from the CAP [Community Action Program] office came and talked to me real good. She said, "We're having a dinner Sunday." And I wanted to cook that dinner and I told her I went over to the CAP office and I said, "Well, I'll help cook." For Aida and Tim. Those we lost. I'll cook for all the people that lost loved ones.

And, I'd like to start some fun and games for the old people. I wanted to start something like that in Allen for the old people. Just forget about everything and let's go and have fun. Doing games, playing games. It would be nice for the old people. But to start something like that in South Dakota it's kind of hard. And, you know, we have meetings and kids say, "We want roller skating and a swimming pool." And, you know, there's no basketball courts for those kids. There are things the kids and the old people need. It would be nice to start something for them.

A few years back, we set up concession at the Pine Ridge powwow. We sell Indian tacos at the powwow. And, we made only six hundred dollars. I got some clothes for the kids. And, I think that we're the only ones that made money, because they all complained about not making money. And, you have to pay four hundred dollars to go in. Before you set up, you're supposed to put up four hundred dollars. We're not supposed to pay that much. Maybe the white people, but not us. That money is supposed to go to the Indian people. We don't have much money—that's why we're working. And here they charge us one hundred dollars a day to set up a table.

A long time ago, we used to put a concession stand in Rosebud. That's where we did it the first time. And we make three thousand dollars that one day! It was easy to make money then. We were all going, working hard! All my girls were working hard. My kids were small then. So they were helping. At the end of the day, I was really tired. Because I was making dough after dough. I had to hire two womens to help me make that dough. Lupe's sister, Cleo, she gets up early and makes stacks and stacks of tortillas. Burritos. And we have fry bread. The concession stands were good then. There were less of them. And, there was a lot of dancers. It was pretty good. You could make your money.

And I think that we try to do our best. To live the Lakota way. And try not to involve money. Money's a big issue! Right now, people talk about charging for ceremony.

LUPE: There was a newspaper article a while back and they said a Sun Dance near Allen charge five thousand dollars. A person!

MELDA: Five thousand dollars a person.

LUPE: I've still got it.

MELDA: They printed a correction. It was in California.

LUPE: Oh, yeah, they did.

MELDA: Something else.

LUPE: There was another article that print all the names of the eastern medicine men, too. They raise questions about them. They've got me in there, too. I'm not a medicine man!

MELDA: That was two women from Kyle doing that. These two women, if they're going to put out something like that, they should just go Sun Dance to Sun Dance.

LUPE: Learn.

MELDA: Be there, see what they're doing. Then they know who's running a good Sun Dance and who's charging. Our Sun Dance we don't charge. I wish it was five thousand dollars. Buy me a four-wheel drive!

LUPE: I'm always working. Sometimes I'm out there by myself and then they come one by one, my sons, my daughters, and my grand-children and they're helping out. And Melda, right behind. She always makes sure she's got everything for us. Sometimes I'm too hard on them. Push them too hard. Because I'm a man, you know, I like to get things done! So I just sit down and my wife she come back to be by me every day.

Me and her we don't argue. Sometimes we just . . .

MELDA: We just fight!

LUPE: Fight one another—fist to fist!! Ho!

MELDA: We started to Sun Dance and it was really hard. Oh, it was hard! The work was very hard for us. But we have to put all that up. And people think we get money out of it, but my dad used to say, "You don't take money." We always just tell everybody to buy groceries. Just go buy whatever. Whatever you can. And a lot of people come back complaining. Grocery prices in Martin are too high! So groceries are important. To have them for sweats, ceremonies.

LUPE: I try to help others. Always feeding people, all the time.

MELDA: So when all those Sun Dancers bring food, it stays down east. Because we have sweats. We've got coffee and we still use it. Lots of coffee!

LUPE: Whatever we got left, we use it.

MELDA: There was a lot of coffee left over. Four large cans. When people come down to sweat, we give them coffee. When Sun Dance comes now, most everyone is off somewhere else. During Sun Dance, people on the reservation are traveling around. They all go to Sun Dances. All over. And powwows. Everything's going on. And they have to be over there. A lot of people make their money that way, going to powwow. And then after Sun Dance they all come back.

LUPE: People come. Because everything is over with. Powwows are over. Sun Dances are over. So they all come. And they all sweat.

MELDA: People come over. They'll say we want to have a sweat on, like, Tuesday. And, sometimes we'll say, "Well, we're taking a sweat tonight." And, they come. You know, when we have sweats, it means I have to cook.

LUPE: So, right away, we start cooking. Make the fire.

MELDA: We make chicken soup. And buy bread. And that's good enough. Make coffee.

LUPE: Sometimes, we have a lot of people there. And everything what I got, you know, I share. Everything, I share. The money. It comes in, it goes out! I told my kids, "Don't be greedy. Try to help people out. Do everything you can, you know, and people will appreciate it. Try to open up your house. Give things away."

A lot of people been selling traditional ways, you know. It's even some of the Lakota people doing that. They go overseas. They do that. They make a lot of money and all that. It's not good at all. You're not supposed to sell the traditional ways at all. When you start selling your traditional way, yourself won't be nothing at all. You'll have done everything for nothing.

And I, myself, a lot of people know me. I never ask for nothing. Like

I always tell people, "I'm not trying to look good. I'm just being the man I am." I don't want to look good and not to be good inside my heart. My heart has got to be good. My clothes aren't going to make me no better than what I am. That's the way it is. I could be a man, I could make a whole lot of money and womens on this traditional way, because I know them all. The ways of the Lakota people. And I could sit down before many people and mislead them. I could do that. I could go up there. I know how to set up an altar and pray like that. People are going to believe me. But who am I going to be fooling? The people. Not *Tunkashila*. And sooner or later he's going to give me payback and I won't like that!

And I know for a fact that I've been put down many time, but I don't care. To me, it doesn't matter. One time, there was a man putting me down. But, then something happen. For some reason, he ask me to sweat lodge. He told me to run it, he said, "Do a sweat for us." So I bring my pipe. And he start crying and said, "There's a man here sitting here who really truly believes." He mentioned my name. "I am sorry," he said, "that I talk about you. Something tell me to tell these things. And I was wrong." People come like that, asking for forgiveness. To me it's all right. For forgiveness: ask him up there. The only man that can give it is up there.

We're only human. We're human beings and we're pitiful. We can try real hard but sometimes we don't talk with our heart, we talk with our tongue. We don't think and our voice comes out. Thinking we're right. So I still got to be learning, you know, to listen and to hear before I talk. I'm a man . . . I'm nobody. I just believe in these ways and good things happen to me. Helping the people. Taking a sweat and I feel good. I try to help people out. As I said, I'm not a medicine man or nothing like that, but I'll help people by building a Sun Dance, the arbors and all that. And teaching them how to pray, you know. The sweat lodge songs. I can sing those. I sing pretty good with my family. Sun Dancers, medicine men, when I pray, they will sing with me.

A lot of good things come into my head, the prayers. There are certain days when I go in a sweat lodge and good things come out of my mouth, good prayers. And, that man, Stanley Looking Horse—you know that medicine man who was taking care of that buffalo camp at Green Grass—told me that I carry strong prayers. When I pray in the sweat lodge. He tell everyone, "This man standing right here is from a different tribe but he carries strong prayers. This man really and truly believes." He liked me pretty well because of the way I prayed. He told Melda and people up there that I carry strong prayers. I don't make nothing up. That make me proud, you know. To hear somebody talk about me like that.

12

Tradition

Traditionalism "symbolizes for the Sioux what it is to be Indian" and has been described in the contemporary era as an "attempt to return to the 'old ways,' the 'traditional ways,' 'Lakota ways' . . . that provide historical links to the past" (DeMallie, "Lakota" 2). While contemporary Lakota identity is often associated with traditional practices, these practices are frequently debated, because an unchanging past is incommensurate with a present that necessitates change. Accordingly, tradition can often be best understood by attending to the pride or, alternatively, reticence that might be associated with specific practices. Anthropologist Raymond DeMallie notes that "[f]or the Lakotas of Pine Ridge . . . to be Lakota, 'Sioux,' or more generally to be *ikcewicasa,* 'common men,' that is, Indians (not whites), is an unwavering source of pride and strength" ("Lakota" 4). In *The Lakota Ritual of the Sweat Lodge: History and Contemporary Practice* (1998), Raymond A. Bucko describes the use of "tradition" and "traditional" in contemporary political and cultural discourses: "Tradition itself is a vital term in contemporary Lakota discourse and constitutes a key symbol in Lakota culture. Tradition is used on the reservation today both as a term to authenticate a legitimate link to the past and as a mark of legitimacy itself. People, behaviors, and ceremonies are often called traditional" (14). He continues: "The word *wichoh'a* 'tradition' is used in several ways by the Lakotas on the reservation. The first meaning matches the English definition of the word; it implies the handing on of a body of material from the past. The second, more analogous to custom or habit, refers to actions in the present that represent generalized repetitive behavior. Finally, the English word *traditional* is used to mean 'proper, correct, or accurate' and can imply one or both of the two Lakota meanings" (98). Because we can speak about tradition as something essential as well as something that has been eroded by colonial forces, individual sentiments about changes in tradition can be both divisive and unifying. Instead of defining "what" constitutes Native tradition, I focus on the individual construction of tradition in contemporary circumstances. How do Native individuals, at present, maintain links to the past? In my approach I follow Bucko's emphasis on the dialectical nature of Lakota ritual and belief as individuals and groups work together "to produce a satisfactory rendition of tradition" (12). "My task is not to establish what is legitimate contemporary practice," he says, "but rather to demonstrate how this legitimacy called tradition is in fact arrived at" (14). Individuals make claims to Lakota tradition in different ways, and these claims are "in turn validated or discredited in various communal and interpersonal contexts" (Pickering, "Review" 186).

Melda talks about peyote as traditional, despite its relatively current introduction, through a demarcation between peyote use and religious traditions associated with non-Native culture. The Native American Church, established in the early 1900s, integrates Christian beliefs, the use of peyote, and, in some churches, the use of the pipe.[1] Melda acknowledges that the use of peyote is not a traditional Lakota practice, since it was adopted from another tribe in the 1900s. "I know that peyote is not traditional," she says. In that sense, she defines "tradition" as that which is pre-colonial. However, peyote use, especially in conjunction with the pipe, contests efforts to suppress Native spiritual practices. It also indicates continued adaptation and innovation of a persistent tradition, namely the use of the pipe. In that sense, Melda speaks with considerable pride about the role of her paternal great-grandfather, Philip Red Bear, in establishing peyote use among the Lakota people, and she describes how he brought peyote from Oklahoma to South Dakota. In *Peyote Religion: A History* (1987) Omer Stewart cites the involvement of Melda's great-grandfather in establishing the pan-Indian syncretic church at several points in his text (87–89, 94–95). He describes Philip Red Bear's use of the traditional Lakota pipe: "The Lakota put their own traditional stamp on the [ceremony] . . . in Red Bear's use of the Pipe" (167). Philip Red

Bear's role in sustaining Lakota spirituality is especially significant given that traditional practices were not supported by government policies at that time. Peyotists began to practice in South Dakota in 1914, and the Native American Church was incorporated in South Dakota in 1922. Currently there are many on the reservation who continue to sustain the Christian sentiments, peyote use, and traditional practices that characterize the Native American Church in South Dakota.

There have necessarily been great costs—both material and emotional—in sustaining religious practices despite external pressures. Generally, we lack information about the "economic and political effects of attempting to continue Lakota ritual practices during the period of cultural suppression by governmental and Christian forces, including denial of food rations and imprisonment" (Pickering, "Review" 186). Melda's paternal great-grandfather was instrumental in bringing the ceremonial use of peyote to South Dakota. The effect of his struggle to resist the suppression of spiritual practices persists today in the historical erosion of their land ownership. Portions of the land "down east" were lost when authorities arrested Philip Red Bear for using peyote; he was put in the position of having to sell part of his land to pay the ensuing legal fees. Land and religion are still very much interconnected for the Lakota people, both politically and culturally. Melda addresses this issue when she talks about the ongoing treaty negotiations that are taking place concerning the Black Hills in South Dakota.[2] She says that it is important to have land so that, in her case, she can raise buffalo, and she often talks of having a herd on the land "down east." Buffalo are used in ceremonial feasts, and their skulls and hides are used as sacred objects. Currently, when Melda holds a Sun Dance she must *purchase* a buffalo to be used for the ceremony. Owning land, therefore, facilitates traditional practices. Inasmuch as land is a political issue for indigenous populations, tradition is also both a cultural and a political issue.[3]

Religious diversity on Pine Ridge Reservation further complicates traditional Lakota beliefs, both historically and in the contemporary context. Raymond DeMallie and Douglas Parks note that "[a]mong some Sioux groups traditional and Christian practices have become amalgamated; among others they are kept strictly separate" (7). At present the reservation is dominated by religious pluralism, whether Christian or Bah'ai or some combination of Lakota beliefs (Bucko 15). For example, Bucko records a Lakota man's description of what he sees as a natural conflation of spiritual beliefs: "These guys who come looking for a pure Indian way of life. They'll see this here picture of Christ and they can't understand it. My grandfather had an altar with his pipe and the statue of Mary. There's one God . . . *Tunkashila* and God are the same. They're just different words, different symbols. So I need both" (175).

I have often been unsettled in much the same way as those guys "looking for a pure Indian way of life" when I have entered houses on Pine Ridge Reservation and found both Christian iconography and Lakota symbols of tradition. In this respect, Melda and Lupe's house is no exception. They adhere to Christian teachings *and* Lakota beliefs and practices. For example, Melda describes her associations to the Christian church, most specifically the Church of God in Scottsbluff, Nebraska. She does not comment on the apparent incompatibility of her adherence to both Christian and traditional beliefs. She focuses instead on prayer and the values she associates with her "life in church." Consequently, social life in the reservation community is also characterized by an attempt to accommodate competing religious beliefs and practices under the more overarching banner of prayer.

Melda makes derisive comments about Catholicism only inasmuch as she aligns the church with colonial practices. More specifically, she counters any efforts to suppress traditional spiritual practices. These associations are evident in a story where she describes the Catholic preacher riding on his horse "down east" and trying to convert her family to Catholicism. She equates this man with colonial imposition: "The *wasicus* came and told them they're going to go to hell if they're not baptized." The Lakota term for "white people" is *wasicu* and has come to mean "'clothes wearers,' 'fat takers,' or 'loud talkers,' emphasizing white men's negative characteristics" (DeMallie, "Lakota" 9).[4] Today the term *wasicu* has come to stand largely as an abstract designation of "a mind-set, a worldview that is a product of the development of European culture" (Means 28). Significantly, Melda also uses the term *wasicu* when talking about the suppression of the Ghost Dance. The Ghost Dance, a ceremony that promises to restore the pre-contact world, was initiated in 1890 by Wovoka, or Jack Wilson (Paiute).[5] It came to the Dakotas in May 1890. The Ghost Dance has been described as a "ritual of militant resistance," and the massacre at Wounded Knee is connected, at least in part, to the threat associated with the ceremony (Rice, *Before* 2). The Ghost Dance was effectively discontinued after the massacre in December 1890 and was only reclaimed in the retraditionalization era of the 1970s and 1980s.[6] It is fitting, then, that Melda uses combative terminology when she describes what has been lost with the erosion of the ceremony.[7] In her narrative she uses *wasicu* when referring to the historical incursion of Lakota spiritual practices; this is the *only* time she uses the term. When she uses *wasicu* in describing the Catholic preacher "down east," she is critiquing Catholicism inasmuch as it is associated with the historical suppression of Native American spirituality and practices.

The cultural renewal that accompanied activist efforts in the 1970s led to a proliferation of cultural and religious practices. Consequently, the number of Sun Dances has increased steadily over the past three decades on Pine Ridge Reservation and elsewhere. Mikael Kurkiala identifies the growing number of Sun Dances on Pine Ridge Reservation: "From the mid 1970s, the number of Sun Dances has grown significantly. . . . In the summer of 1993, approximately thirty Sun Dances were held on different locations on the Pine Ridge and Rosebud Reservations. In the summer of 1997, the number had increased to 43 on Pine Ridge alone" (227). In 1979 several hundred people attended the tribal Sun Dance at Porcupine (Steinmetz 79). However, as the number of Sun Dances increases, the number of people attending each Sun Dance and the number of medicine men who can run each Sun

Dance decreases dramatically. In 2000, including the memorial Sun Dance honoring Lupe Trejo, there were at least three simultaneous Sun Dances in the immediate area of Allen alone. These ceremonies are held for a four-day period scheduled anytime throughout the entire summer period; the simultaneous ceremonies are therefore quite significant.

Given the increase in the number of Sun Dances, the competition over "viable" ceremonies accelerates due to greater opportunities for comparison and also because there are simply fewer available medicine men to run the ceremonies. The dialectic surrounding authentic ceremonies is, in part, a corollary to the proliferation of traditional practices and the ongoing discourse surrounding correct practices. In *American Indian Ethnic Renewal: Red Power and the Resurgence of Identity and Culture* (1996) Joane Nagel says, "[i]ndividual Indian ethnic renewal appears to be tightly connected to an interest and a participation in tribal traditions and ceremonial practices" (190). She also acknowledges the contested nature of traditional practices in the contemporary context: "Despite the well-known fact that identities and cultures change, . . . document[ing] the reconstruction, much less the new construction of an individual's ethnic identity or a community's cultural practices or institutions, is often an unwelcome, sometimes vilified enterprise" (63).

Current Sun Dances maintain continuity with the past and also necessarily incorporate more recent changes. Spiritual practitioners must balance traditional and contemporary needs, and interpretations as to how that balance is best achieved vary among individuals and communities. For example, there are debates on Pine Ridge Reservation about whether non-Native people should be allowed to take part, since some believe that Sun Dances are "more" traditional if only Lakota participants are involved. In this sense, that which is "traditional" is defined through its resistance to a colonial presence. At the same time, individuals on the reservation, Melda and Lupe included, advocate that allies, or relations, are meant to pray together.[8] Melda and Lupe welcome dancers and supporters of any racial or tribal designation at their Sun Dance. They have done so since the beginning of their Sun Dance, but their actions have taken on new meaning since the debate surrounding cultural legitimacy emerged on the reservation.⁹ When she talks about the Sun Dance, Melda advocates that no one should be excluded from the ceremony. Her view is based on traditional Lakota teachings on forming alliances and honoring relations. She refers to different races, such as "white people, black people" as well as "different kinds of Indians," and cites her father and medicine man Ruben Fire Thunder in addressing the issue. She says that praying "with everybody" is "the only way you're going to heaven." She disengages from the racial aspects of the debate by instead urging a spiritual understanding of human nature: the claiming of relations through prayer.

Prayer operates in part through the understanding of *Wakan Tanka* as something that is unknowable. *Wakan Tanka*, generally glossed as meaning "god," is the sum of all that is mysterious and sacred, or *wakan*. Anthropologist Beatrice Medicine (Lakota) says, "*Wakan Tanka* translates from the Lakota language to mean 'Great Holy' or 'Great Spirit' or 'God'" (qtd. in Harjo and Bird 208). *Tunkashila*, meaning "grandfather," is often referred to as a personification of *Wakan Tanka* (see Rice, *Before* 146). *Wakan* has been described as "anything that was hard to understand" and is often associated with sacred power (Walker, *Belief* 70). DeMallie and Parks describe a belief in *wakan* as the "basis of the Lakotas' culturally distinctive theory of existence" (8). Julian Rice defines *wakan* as "cosmic energy obtained through personal visions" (*Before* 21). Holy men (*wacasa wakan*) and women (*winyan wakan*) connect through their personal experiences with *wakan*, but access to that which is sacred is not restricted to traditional practitioners. Prayer and ceremony facilitate spiritual knowledge among all individuals in the Lakota community.

From a traditional Lakota perspective, identity involves knowing one's relationship to the divine, *wakan*, which is in all relations. Consequently, Lakota spiritual beliefs and practices provide a theoretical framework for understanding the world. Lakota storyteller and singer Severt Young Bear elaborates on the implications for Lakota identity:

> Our Lakota people understand some things. Identity is based on the idea of slolic'iya, knowing who you are. In connection with that is the notion that there are limits, of only going so far, of having a limit. Around us there's an aura, a barrier that goes around us, a limit of our being. To get beyond that to the universe and the Great Spirit, we use our voice, we throw our voice loud and clear, we get on top of a hill and throw our voice in prayer. In this way we hope to find ourselves. It used to work, but now it takes a special effort to succeed. (106)

In this passage, Young Bear refers to going to the top of a hill, which is a way of describing the vision quest (*hambleceya*). He describes "throwing a voice," which means "to pray": "*Ho ye waye'lo nama'hon ye wani' ktelo'* / A voice I am sending, hear me, I will live" (Densmore 124).[10] Similarly, in *The Sacred Pipe: Black Elk's Account of the Seven Rites of the Oglala Sioux,* Black Elk says: "Grandfather, I am sending a voice! To the Heavens of the universe, I am sending a voice; That my people may live!" (J. E. Brown 53).[11] Young Bear describes throwing a voice, or prayer, and says, "[i]n this way we hope to find ourselves." In this sense, praying ensures that the people "will live"—that *all* that exists will continue to be related and that one's position among these relations will be sustained.

The traditional Lakota conception of identity is grounded in an epistemological tradition that both differentiates between and encompasses mainstream theories of selfhood. According to traditional Lakota beliefs, all relations are sacred. The act of prayer maintains these relationships. Knowing who you are, or claiming an individual identity, necessarily also involves claiming sacred knowledge. Accordingly, Dakota scholar Elizabeth Cook-Lynn says that the "question '*taku iniciapi he?*' or 'what is your name' is a sacred question which most often means 'who are you in relation to all the rest of us?'" (Gonzalez and Cook-Lynn 189). By interacting with others about what constitutes tradition, as well as with *Tunkashila* and *Wakan Tanka*, individuals are enacting tradition and "co-creating the world." The *relationship* to *Tunkashila* and *Wakan Tanka* is what determines meaning in Lakota tradition. In the next chapter, Lupe talks about this relationship. He says, "[p]ray to yourself and talk. *Tunkashila* and *Wakan Tanka* know what you're there for." He goes on to say, "I truly believe what's in there [the sweat lodge ceremony], is what you put in there." And elsewhere in his narrative he stresses that one must pray with "a good heart and a good mind." This spiritual understanding undercuts the distinction between faith and reason, right and wrong, black and white. Decisions are sovereign and sacred because each individual is part of all that is related. Accordingly, the prayer *Mitakuye 'oyasin* ("All My Relations") is a way of invoking and sustaining the sacredness associated with what are, from a traditional Lakota perspective, the divine relations among all things.

13

These Old People Pray Real Good

MELDA: When I was growing up, the boys did some sweats. With the Crow Dogs. When I first met him, Leonard Crow Dog was a small boy. Leonard always go around with my brother, Norman. You know, when we go to pick potatoes, he used to go too. In Nebraska—Scottsbluff. I guess my brothers, Junior and Norman, they start having sweats with Leonard. They used to have a lot of sweats back then. That's when they started. And their dad used to build sweat lodges. Henry Crow Dog. So they did sweats a long time ago. Before all these other people started having sweats over here.

When I first started going to sweats, I sort of sit outside and pray. With Ruben Fire Thunder. I watched the door, opened the door. Sometimes, I take rocks in. But he didn't do sweats with womens, just mens. And I used to take the rocks in. And then I graduate to watching the door. That was when my mom was alive. My mom used to pray in ceremony, but not in the sweat. She didn't go in because it was only for men. We didn't have mixed sweats until after Ruben died. Sometimes, you know, if Ruben's wife, Pansy, runs it, we womens could go in. That's not all the time. Once in a while. She said, "I'll run it." And everybody was real happy to go in because she was going to run it. And Ruben sits outside. He sit outside and we all sing—of course I didn't sing at the time. All those old people, sing. And the spirits go in. Yeah. That's really something. I experienced something. It was real good. And, Ruben kind of surprised me sometimes. We sit outside and Pansy pray, and my mom pray. And sometimes he tells me to pray. And I said, "Oh, I'll say a little, short prayer." Because I know those old people pray real good and I learned a lot from old people. Pansy and my mom. So they pray and then he always told me to come to the door and pray too. So I started out watching the door and then sometimes when nobody was there I take the rocks in. So

I learn from way at the bottom. You gotta slowly work yourself up. Traditional ways, I think, you have to go . . .

LUPE: Sit down and talk. Talk to the people.

MELDA: Start from way on the bottom and learn as you go. Slowly. Like first grade, kindergarten, first grade. To me, you cannot just go in and learn everything. As you go along, it's hard. It's really hard. Sometimes I feel like I don't have nothing to do with anything!

LUPE: Me, I been on *hambleceya* a few times now. If I say I'm going to *hambleceya* for four days, then I do it four days, regardless, no matter what. I make sure I stay up there. The first time I *hambleceya*—it's not because I wanted to. No. Something was bothering me. It seemed like I was losing myself. Something in my head, something holding me. And I went to work in the days all the time and I told Melda about it. So I went to see Ruben Fire Thunder, the medicine man, and I told him, I explained it to him. He said, "Brother, the time has come to you to do a *hambleceya*. That is why you're like that." And I said, "Okay."

The thing that was bothering me, I see people in the dark. When I was outside, down east, I seen things. I see people walking. Tall ones. Short ones. Women. Men. I seen it. And I seen a man. It was getting kind of dark and all of a sudden I saw a man; a tall man right there. But, he went home because the little ones were outside. It bothered me like that. He told me: "Those people have come for you. You've been dancing for many years now and you haven't gone up on the hill. Those spirits have come to you now. They want you up there."

When I got ready, Ruben told everybody . . . Melda heard this, everybody heard it: "There's going to be a lot of people there. And there's going to be an old man and woman coming." He didn't mention names. "An old man and an old woman are gonna come." Everybody listened to him. He keeps saying that.

MELDA: There were a lot of old people alive then and my aunt was the one that brought the three kinds of *wasna*. And *wojapi*. Lupe went up there for the elders. That was for his mom. And, for the old people. To go up on that hill. A lot of elders came. And my aunt said, "Nobody never *hambleceya* for the elders. It's always for themselves." She was real happy he did that. And, they brought a lot of food.

LUPE: And an old man and an old woman came. Out of nowhere. They appeared at the door. Knock at the door.

MELDA: That old woman brought a pound of coffee and a big piece of meat. Kidney. She told me, she said, "I didn't cook it. So go ahead and keep it for some other time." She brought a big meat and coffee. This old lady I never did see.

LUPE: Everybody sit down in a circle. We were ready. And they sit down way in a corner over there. They sit there. I remember because I was sitting right there facing them. There was a man and a woman. When we pray, they pray really good.

MELDA: The old man brought his pipe. And they sit there. You know when you go in the ceremony and everybody prays, he prayed real good for us. And then after we eat, and after everything, those two just walk out. "We're going home now." They *didn't* say, "We'll see you." They said, "We're going now." And those two old people left—they went out. And . . .

LUPE: They didn't have no car.

MELDA: I don't know if they came in a car or not. They just went out of the house.

LUPE: We didn't hear no car leaving.

MELDA: After they left, after they went out the door, we were all sitting just finishing up and talking. And pretty soon my mom said, "Who are those two?" I said, "I don't know. Do you know them? You're from here." And then my aunt says, "Do you know them?" And they said, "I never did see those two people. Where are they from?"

LUPE: The medicine man didn't know them either.

MELDA: And we ask him. And all those old people ask each other, "Who's that man and woman?" Nobody knows. And that was funny because nobody talked to them. You know when you go into something—hypnotized. I guess we were all like that inside because we didn't pay attention to who they were. You know when you go visit someone and you ask, "Where are you from? Who are you?" Nobody did ask.

LUPE: Nobody did ask.

MELDA: So we were hypnotized until they went out and then everybody start asking, "Who are those people?"

LUPE: Not even Ruben knew them. But he told us that two old people were coming. He knew that.

MELDA: He said, "Did you remember that, before the ceremony, I said there was going to be a man and woman there?"

LUPE: They were there.

MELDA: So we really experienced a lot of good things like that. Oh yeah, and that fire start by itself four times! Before the *hambleceya*, we have sweats for four days. The four days we're going to have a sweat, the fire starts by itself. This was right before he was gonna go *hambleceya*. That was really something good. A lot of people went there. We had sweats every evening. And, before he went up the hill, they set it up.

LUPE: We were coming down to the sweat lodge. Me, Eugene Reddest, of course Ruben. And we saw the sweat lodge and we could see a blue light. And then a big cloud came from the north. A big black one. Thunder and all that. Bad.

MELDA: So we all run in the house.

LUPE: We run in the house. Then we go out. Start the fire.

MELDA: Ruben said, "Just set it up and the fire will go by itself. You don't need a match or anything." I didn't believe him. And my brother, Junior, didn't believe it. A lot of us didn't believe it. So we were going to start the fire for the rocks for the sweat lodge. We cleaned it out. We went over there and, what they did, was they took that broom and they clean it out. Everything. They check it out, so there was no ashes in there. It was just dirt. So he set it up again. And we all sit around.

We all sit around and we just watch because we didn't believe. I kind of didn't believe it either.

LUPE: You had your doubts.

MELDA: Yes, well, it is something that you have to see. So we all sit around there and they set it up.

LUPE: Pretty soon it start smoking. The wind was hard but the flame was straight up.

MELDA: It start from in the middle. Right in the middle, there's a little smoke coming up by itself. And then all of a sudden like someone just pour kerosene in there, pretty soon, all around there, it just took off. Real fast.

LUPE: Like somebody put gas around it and light a match.

MELDA: Yeah!

LUPE: Boom!

MELDA: All of a sudden: "Pow!" And that whole thing . . . and everybody looked at each other: "How did that thing happen?"

Ruben was like that. He was a medicine man. He never flirt with women. Women sit over there and talk and the men sit over here and talk. So when we go over there we just sit outside and pray. We have sweats. He would say, "I'm going to let my spirits go in. And my spirits will pour the water." His spirits poured the water. You could feel that cup on you and the water was sprinkling. Sprinkles. Like when the water comes down. And it doesn't burn you. They was careful and they know what they're doing. And some of that water would go to you. Cold water would go to you. And he said, "Just leave it. Just pray." So that's what we did. And the water went all around. And then on the last round, he don't pour all the water. In the end, the water was all gone. So that's really something. I experience a lot of good things.

I was in there with my mom, Pansy, and other old women. And they pray real good and the prayers were short. Not real long.

LUPE: Pray to yourself and talk. *Tunkashila* and *Wakan Tanka* know what you're there for.

MELDA: They know what you need.

LUPE: But people go on and on. I do that sometimes too, you know.

MELDA: That's the way. You don't get into these things right away. You've got to wait until you're ready and when they're ready.

LUPE: Ruben Fire Thunder told me eagle feathers have to be earned. You've got to earn these feathers. Going out hunting, you bring in meat, buffalo, food for the people, and you earn a feather. You go out there, you know. War and all that. They give you a feather. When you come back. You have to earn the right to have a staff. My staff only got a bundle of tobacco on it.

MELDA: But people are going to do what they're going to do.

LUPE: Yeah.

MELDA: You know, I had something real good happen to me recently. At Sun Dance something really nice, good happened. My mom's pipe was brought back by a family that had it. And I asked the old people about how we're going to do the pipe. And they told us, "Use that pipe for the Sun Dance because it's your mom's pipe. So go in with that pipe. If you have grandkids, you know, every day, the *winyan*, girls, could go in with the pipe." And, I said, "Okay, that's what we're going to do." So that's what happened and the last day, I go in. I said, "I'm going in with it because I stood here and watched all my grandkids in there piercing." I always ask for strength. And I really did, kind of, feel good about it. Taking that pipe in. It was hard, but . . .

LUPE: It was her first time dancing. First time.

MELDA: First time. I said, "Grandma, what did you do to me?! You got me into this, with your pipe!" First time. It is hard work. But it turned out good. Over the last few years, all my kids, all my grandkids Sun Danced. I think, every year one of my grandkids go in.

And, one day during that Sun Dance, there was an eagle flying around. This was before I went in dancing. I was looking at that eagle. I was thinking to myself, "You know, that's real nice feathers. I wish

I could have one." And here that eagle was flying over me and took off. So, later that evening, I went to the house with my granddaughter and we took that red van and went out for some things. And here I opened that door and that eagle feather was there. I opened the door to the van and that eagle feather was on the seat. *Real good*. So that's when I decided: "Well, I'm going to go in with my mom's *chanupa* the last day." First time I dance. First time. And I ask Uncle Tom. I said, "I got this eagle feather." I said, "Uncle Tom, I don't know what to do with it." I ask him, "Uncle Tom, what am I going to do with this feather?" And he said, "Melda," he said, "I think your mom gave you that eagle feather. You take it in and you pray for the elderlies and you pray for good health for the people." And I ask, "Who's going to keep the feather?" He said, "You know, Lupe was really sick last year. He had cancer. What you could do is pierce with it. And give it to Lupe. You let him keep the feather in the family." So all these things I ask the elderlies. What to do? I take advice from the elderlies. That's what happened to me last year.

So all the things I do, I ask the old people what to do. I never do these things myself. I always sit down and talk to the old people: "How come this? And what am I supposed to do?" That's the way I learn.

LUPE: My uncle, Uncle Tom, told me a lot of good things, a lot of good things. He said, "What we've done here, Lupe, these are the right places and the right times of the year to come when people get together and pray. And everybody lives with a good heart and good thoughts. There's good medicine here. The medicine here it's just like the truth. The medicine will always be here. And that medicine is here for the people." My uncle told me these things. When I sit down with old people, like Uncle Tom, he talks. And Ruben talks to me. Put real good things in my head and all that.

You know, people go to the Sun Dance and they see good things. One year, some dancers saw a man out there on the east side looking at the dance. I didn't see it myself, but a lot of people seen it. Yellow, black and white. A clown. *Heyoka*. They seen it. We sit down and we talk to Uncle Tom and say, "Tell me about it." He said, "The spirits are here and they're coming to you, because you're doing something good." When I tell him I want to go look, he said, "No, leave it alone. Don't look for nothing. You're supposed to leave it alone." I pray. I said, "Hau!" That's what I said!

MELDA: "Hau." That's good.

Traditional ways are really strong, because when my granddaughter, Juanita, got into that wreck and she was not going to walk. Bad wreck because it broke her spine. So we went over there and we see her in the hospital. And she looked at me and I got her by the hand and I prayed. And told her, "You'll be all right." So they took her upstairs and they give her all kinds of test. They said her neck was broken. Her spine was broken. We stayed with her. We did a lot of praying for her. We went up the hill. We took flags up there and we took the *chanupa*.

LUPE: We went to a hill and we took tobacco and prayers up there. It was me, all the girls, Melda, Norman, Cleo. All up there. We pray. We left tobacco in the tree.

MELDA: Later, when Juanita was recovering, she saw Manuel, my son, the one that died. She said he came and sat on the bed. He said, "You'll be all right." He said, "You'll be all right, Juanita. I just came to tell you, you're all right." And he smiled. And she said, "Manuel looked really good. He smiled." Then, the phone ring. She couldn't move out of the bed. But, somehow she got the phone. Because he hand it to her. He said, "I'll get it for you." And he put it beside the bed. So she picked up that phone and put it to her head and the nurse came in and my son disappeared.

LUPE: The nurse got scared how that phone got there. She said, "How did that phone get there?"

You know, my granddaughter, she could have been paralyzed. We pray hard. And I think our prayers were answered because a day later she wanted to walk.

MELDA: She wanted to get up and walk. She wasn't supposed to be able to walk. We were all there and the nurses were there and the doctors. And she said, "I want to walk." And they told her, "You can't walk." And I told them, "Let her walk, if she wants to walk. Let her try." So she did. She got up. They help her up, real slow. She sit there and then she got up. And she walked.

LUPE: By herself.

MELDA: She start walking out the door and down the aisle. And the doctors and nurses come. And Lupe start crying.

LUPE: It was amazing. My tears coming down because I seen her walking.

MELDA: The prayers are strong. So what she did a year later, was her thanksgiving. When we have Sun Dance, she did her *wopila*, her thanksgiving. She danced and she pierced. That was the *wopila* they had. You have to do it if you get well.

LUPE: She did it all by herself.

MELDA: I didn't say, "Juanita, you have to do your *wopila*. Because this is the way you do it if we all pray for you." She just said, "Grandma, I'm going to dance." When I got there, she was dancing and she pierced. She did her *wopila*. That was really nice. I said, "I'm really glad. That's a load off Lupe's back. I'm really glad you did all that by yourself."

LUPE: Our prayers have been answered many, many times. Like I tell people, "When you pray, pray with a good heart and a good mind. Leave all worries behind. You come in the arbor or in the sweat, you leave them outside. There's always going to be a time to pick it up again." My brother, Ruben Fire Thunder, told me, he said, "Brother, I tell this to my people all the time. When you have a bad feeling going into a sweat lodge, *hambleceya*, to a Sun Dance, if you've got a bad feeling then don't go. Stay home and live with yourself and your bad feelings. Save them from other people who are trying to do good." And he's right. I've seen that many, many times.

Our traditional ways are really powerful. And you truly believe on it, everything is possible, it will happen, your prayers will be answered. With the traditional ways. I truly believe what's in there, is what you put in there. The grandfathers, they're going to be there for you. *Tunkashila* will come down and make sure that the rocks are there with you and are blessed with the water. And you, yourself, sitting there as a human being to change your life with your heart. To pray with it. *Wakan Tanka* and the rocks and *Tunkashila*. The rocks, you offer for them and not for us. *Tunkashila* is going to bless you right there. And so all these things combined are the traditional ways of the Lakota people. A lot of people misuse it. I tell people many times, "When you go in a sweat lodge, respect yourself and respect others, prepare yourself when you go in there." Like, I tell people, my belief is the red road, when you're there I want everyone to get together and have a good celebration. Pray for one another, eat with one another, work with one another.

MELDA: We went over to Green Grass, where they have the pipe, and talked with Stanley Looking Horse. Lupe talked with him. The men sit over there and talk and the women sit over here. Oh, I learned a lot.

When we got there, Lupe gave a pipe to Stanley Looking Elk. We went over to the sweat lodge. And it was really powerful. It was like a lot of spirits came in and the eagle came in. You know how hot the sweat lodge is? That eagle came in and it was cool. The wings make it cool. I experience that. It was really something. And, on the last round when he pour all the water on the rocks, it looks like all those rocks were talking in Indian. In the old language that I don't understand. It was really nice.

The men talk. Go out for medicine. I talk with his wife. I ask questions. I ask her about the pipe. I ask when they brought the pipe. She said that when Jesus came, that's when that woman brought that pipe. That's *very* interesting. They always say in the books: five hundred years ago. But this is longer than that. She told me, "When they first brought that pipe, it's got two red eagle feathers." She said, "A long time ago, Lakotas, long long time ago, there were red eagles. And there's two red eagle feathers on that pipe." That was something I learned. Me, I ask questions. I say, "Why?"

You can't see that pipe because it's wrapped in buffalo robe. It takes care of itself. It's very powerful. That's the way they talk about that pipe. My uncle Poor Thunder was a medicine man that smoked that pipe, saw that pipe. My mom told me about that. She said she went with them. And she was very young, she said. So years and years later I went to Green Grass.

When we went over I was thinking that it would be nice if all the Indian people get together and go there. All those medicine men should—well, this is my way of thinking—they should go over there before they Sun Dance and they should all go pray and then come and do all the Sun Dances. That would be really nice.

So we learned from the old people. We don't just go and do this and that.

LUPE: Don't make nothing up.

MELDA: We have to talk to the old people. We went to Ruben Fire Thunder. And Earl Swift Hawk.

LUPE: And, now, Sam Moves Camp. That's a good man, right there. Sam Moves Camp comes and help. When we need something, he comes to my home, sit down, and we talk. Have long talks. Even when Melda's not around. He's really a nice man to talk to. Head down. If you're serious about something, he'll sit down and talk to you about it. That's a man who truly believe in his ways.

MELDA: Sam Moves Camp is young. He's not old. He's younger than us.

LUPE: He's fifty-four.

MELDA: Fifty-four.

LUPE: But he's got a lot of gray hair.

MELDA: He's got a lot of kids. He's got eight kids. I was surprised. He's real skinny. He's young.

LUPE: That man could tease you to death!

MELDA: Oh, yeah. He teases. A while back, Sam Moves Camp was real busy helping with Sun Dance. Different Sun Dances. And, they bring rocks from Rapid City. He didn't go back to his house for two days. So Lupe was helping him and . . . this was funny . . . his wife came for him. I said, "He's not here." I says, "He took off to Rapid." Working hard. Later on, he tells us, "My wife asked me 'Where have you been all these days?' I say, 'I was with Lupe. She said, '*What*?!!'" Oh, she took it the wrong way. She thought he meant, "I was *with* Lupe." He tell us this when we have that dinner and everyone sits around and joke and talk. And he was joking around. She thought he was *with* Lupe. Oh, that was funny. We laughed.

LUPE: When Sam brought me a pipe, he came to our home. Melda was not around, so he sit down, smoke a cigarette, drink some coffee. He got up. You know what he did?! He got the broom. And he start sweeping all the rooms. He was housecleaning! He clean the whole house. The cups and all that. Traditional. He's that kind of man—medicine man. He said, "I'm gonna come tonight. I'll bring the medicine." He brought medicine. And, we eat. Eat, pray, eat. He served the old people, he served himself. He don't sit down, you know. He help everybody. He eats with the people and he jokes with the people. That's a man that loves the people. A medicine man that thinks about the people. Treats people in a respectable way. To understand each other and communicate in a good way.

14

Knowledge

The issue of protecting indigenous knowledge is "associated with larger Native American pressures for sovereignty—cultural, political, and intellectual" (Whiteley 4). Appropriation is implicated in cross-cultural collaborations because culture can be commodified, detached from intended contexts, and used as capital in a number of intellectual and economic markets. Dakota scholar Vine Deloria Jr. comments on the disparity that perpetuates the exchange across cultures:

> Much of the difficulty that Indians have today with the appropriation of Indian rituals and teachings is the superior attitude which non-Indians project, once they have made some acquaintance with things Indian. In most cases they have a sneering, self-righteous posture which communicates the message, to Indians and non-Indians alike, that they know all about Indian religion. . . . The non-Indian appropriator conveys the message that Indians are indeed a conquered people and there is nothing that Indians possess, absolutely nothing—pipes, dances, land, water, feathers, drums, and even prayers—that non-Indians cannot take whenever and wherever they wish. . . . Indians are therefore put in a position where we must share with others—everything—but they need not share with us. (*For* 265)

I have ideological and personal investments, as well as a responsibility to stakeholders, in both academic and Native communities. Consequently, I have negotiated the tensions over how authority is constructed in each sphere. This necessarily has implications for a project that involves cultural knowledge. As Linda Tuhiwai Smith (Kaupapa Maori) asks, "To who is the researcher accountable?" (173).

In the academic community, concerns over ethics and research protocols have developed alongside indigenous concerns over appropriation. Universities, government funding agencies, and tribal governments have made efforts to establish policies to ensure that research is conducted ethically.[1] In order to protect cultural property, many tribes require that academic researchers obtain permission from their tribal council. The Hopis are well known for their tribal ethics review, as Peter M. Whiteley describes in *Rethinking Hopi Ethnography* (1998). The Hopi governing body will "take at least a year to consider research projects and then may not approve them" ("Native"). Accordingly, the academy requires that researchers follow institutional review board (IRB) protocols in conducting research. Although there are at present debates around whether oral history work should be required to follow these procedures, my own research followed IRB guidelines.

As an academic interviewing "human subjects," I was required to submit a Request for Ethical Review to the Office of Research Services at the University of British Columbia (the IRB for this project). I decided that obtaining consent from the governing tribal body was the most ethical way to ensure that my research was valuable to the Lakota community, and I devised what I regarded as suitable ethics forms. I designed two forms in 1997, one for those I was interviewing, the other to be signed by the Oglala Sioux (Lakota) Tribal Council. Melda and Lupe signed their consent forms and, at that time, told me that Pine Ridge Reservation is too large and complex to allow for the involvement of the tribal council in such projects. Knowing Melda and Lupe as I do, I trust their understanding of the protocols on the reservation. However, I was also accountable to the university and to the policies I had originally outlined. Academic authorities prompted me to inquire, both verbally and in writing, about research protocols with the Oglala Sioux Office of the Tribal President, the Oglala Sioux Office of the Secretary, and the Oglala Sioux Tribal Office. To confirm my understanding about vetting proposals, I sent a registered letter to the tribal offices. In finding there to be no formal policies in place with the Oglala Sioux Tribal Council (2001), I realized that it was a mistake to assume uniformity across different tribes and that institutional ethics policies could benefit from an increased capacity to anticipate and respond to this diversity.[2] After attending to the university recommendations, I called Melda and, among other things, told her about contacting the tribal council. In reply, she told me a humorous story about police officers on the reservation: that they *know better* than to bother someone like herself with unnecessary road checks and, therefore, leave her to govern herself. I interpret this as being a story about Melda's experiences with conventional authority figures and her effort to teach me about different ways of conceiving of power, authority, and accountability.

Traditional governance was in place prior to the formation of the elected tribal council and involves *tiyospaye*, or kin groups. The traditional *tiyospaye* structure involves a series of interconnections, albeit with elders as authorities. Patricia Albers states that "[t]o a large extent, tribal politics and domestic politics are the same. The social formations which dominate the everyday life of most Sioux are defined by kinship and organized around the interests of separate but related domestic groups or *tiospaye* [*sic*])" ("Sioux" 216). The present tribal political structure of an elected political leadership is distinct from interrelated *tiyospaye* groups, and this change in structure has resulted in necessary shifts in power.[3] Nonetheless, Lakota religious leadership has a long history and, in many ways, continues to function in the reservation community. Accordingly, Melda and Lupe have ways of authorizing a project in the Lakota community that do not necessitate the involvement of the tribal council. Melda often talks about the importance of asking questions of elder Lakota members of the tribe. She stresses the importance of asking questions about matters that involve the community, ceremony, and tradition. She says, "Me, I ask questions, I say, 'Why?'" In her life story, Melda describes how she received an eagle feather. She asked an elder about the sacred object: "And I asked Uncle Tom. I said, 'I got this eagle feather.' I said, 'Uncle Tom, I don't know what to do with it.' . . . So all these things I ask the elderlies. What to do? I take advice from the elderlies." Melda indicates that elders or religious leaders should always be consulted about tribal issues, and in the few instances when she has told me a story that extends beyond her own life, she has consulted what she regards as the proper religious/tribal authorities for permission. She is following what she understands as traditional Lakota ethical practices. Tuhiwai Smith says that traditional ethical practices are meant to answer questions such as "Is her spirit clear? Does he have a good heart?" (10). Lupe echoes this sentiment; he says, "Like I tell people, 'When you pray, pray with a good heart and a good mind.'" Melda and Lupe describe ethics as associated with traditional and religious authorities, and their understanding of the project proceeds along those lines.

At one point in my research, a scholar asked, "Have Melda and Lupe prayed for this project?" I could only answer, "Not in any way that I can prove." I have indicated that Melda and Lupe have followed traditional Lakota practices for ensuring the ethics of their project. How do I know this? How can I prove this? I cannot *prove* traditional ethical practices to the academic community, because there is no way of directly explaining Lakota religious authority outside of the Lakota religious context. In *Prison Writings* (1999), Leonard Peltier (Lakota) says that he cannot provide details of his experiences inside the sweat lodge (*inipi*): "This precaution is for your sake as much as mine. To speak of what happens to me in the *inipi* would be like giving *you* the medicine intended for *me*. It would be pointless, even harmful—to you as well as to me" (197). I have repeatedly witnessed Melda and Lupe in the act of prayer, but I have also learned that silences around sacred matters, at times, carry considerable authority. Writing about religious approval in an academic forum is difficult because academic writing requires evidence (see Giltrow 72–74). I do not understand the concept of Lakota religious power (*wakan*) or medicine (*pejuta*) well enough to *know* what I can and cannot disclose about sacred matters. I have provided evidence that I am unable to prove spiritual authority in an academic context, and I hope that this project may instead serve, in part, as a forum for learning how these two realms of experience—sacred and academic—might be more compatible and mutually informing.

Sometimes, not speaking about spiritual matters is the best way to honor sacred knowledge.[4] For example, I learned that silences can often occur around particular subjects. Specifically, my own conversations with Melda and Lupe about Crazy Horse demonstrate this kind of exchange. Crazy Horse is associated with a particular history on the reservation. In 1874, gold was discovered in the Black Hills and tensions arose from settler competition for the land that led to armed conflict. Crazy Horse took part in several of these battles. In 1877, Crazy Horse surrendered at Fort Robinson. He was renowned for his skills as a warrior and was killed upon his surrender at the fort, presumably for political reasons. Crazy Horse represents a larger context of Lakota traditionalism and resistance to oppression. Wounded Knee and the Battle of Little Bighorn are also part of this legacy.[5] These events, and the figures associated with them, represent injustice and loss as well as resistance and endurance. For this reason, Crazy Horse is spoken of quite frequently on the reservation, even in the contemporary period. Specifically, Melda had mentioned Crazy Horse in describing her disapproval over the representation of his love life in a recent television movie about the celebrated warrior:

MELDA: Yeah. He's [Crazy Horse] not married. The other girl died. He's probably turning around in his grave, wanting to come out and straighten us all out.

LARISSA: Yeah. Wherever his grave is. . . .

LUPE: Same thing like Custer. They say that Custer hated Indians. He didn't hate them. He likes Indians. He even got married to one of them. Married to a Cheyenne woman.

This exchange, to me, shows some aspects of Lakota knowledge and ethics. The location of Crazy Horse's grave site is considered sacred knowledge. Queries as to whether its location is known and, if so, if it can be revealed are debated on the reservation.[6] I suspect that Melda and Lupe know the location of Crazy Horse's burial site. In *To Kill an*

Eagle: Indian Views on The Last Days of Crazy Horse (1981), Howard Red Bear (1871–1968) talks about Crazy Horse. His father, Melda's great-grandfather, is the third cousin of Crazy Horse (Kadlecek 139, 161). Howard Red Bear says that Crazy Horse's father left with the body but nobody knows where it is buried. He alludes to the fact that Crazy Horse may be buried somewhere near the Beaver Creek area (155). In our conversation, I was trying to obtain information about this aspect of Lakota discourse. However, when I raise this topic, Lupe changes the subject and none of us pursue the discussion further. I regard this as an example of the ethics around disclosing sacred knowledge as well as Melda and Lupe's efforts to teach me about proper practices.

Melda and Lupe also talked about a particular historical event involving General Custer at one point in our conversations. The Battle of Little Bighorn took place on June 25, 1876, when Cheyennes and Lakotas defeated Custer and the Seventh Cavalry. I have omitted the discussion we had about this battle, and it is one of the few instances when I have made this kind of editorial decision. When Melda and Lupe talked about this battle they were talking about a matter that extends beyond their own lives. Nonetheless, Melda conveyed her personal knowledge of the event by explaining a Lakota word that has taken on specific meanings that relate to the battle. She demonstrated that she found validity in a historical account through a complex understanding of language. Later on, when the narratives were being written up, I accompanied Melda when she asked a member of the community about passing on this story. I realized afterward that, while Melda was given permission, my own role in adhering to traditional ethical practices was not fully realized. The feeling of security that Melda attained could not be achieved in my own experience, because I did not understand enough about consulting directly with traditional authorities. Consequently, the content of the exchange seems less important, in this instance, than the process of witnessing and learning from Melda about her obligation to traditional authorities and my own gradual learning about what I both know and do not know about these processes.

Many of Melda and Lupe's stories depict their individual processes of learning—about tradition, about family, and about their own sense of themselves. In particular, Melda's stories often revolve around her experiences in not knowing about something. Accordingly, there is one particular story—one that she tells very frequently—that I have interpreted and reinterpreted on several occasions in the course of my own learning. It is about her grandson Patrick taking part in his first Sun Dance. I have heard the story many times in different contexts and continue to find in it new meanings. When Patrick was very young he wanted to dance in the Sun Dance ceremony, and he knew that he had to have a Sun Dance skirt in order to dance. Melda relates the discussion that she has with both her mother and her daughter Barbara about this event. She speaks in a lighthearted tone and tends to laugh quietly at many points in the story. Here is that story:

MELDA: You know, I want to talk on how Patrick, my grandson, started Sun Dancing. This is back when we started Sun Dance. My mom was there. And, I had all my kids there. We were all there. And I had my son, the one that died, was there too. He came and he was always helping out. He was always around there, helping out. And the first year was really good. And that's when my grandson Patrick started. First year. Yeah, and he was only like three and a half years old. And he was into the sweats. He was only going in with Grandma and Lupe and all those old people. So he was really interested in this. He was just a little boy, but he was interested. Just like he was peeking in there saying, "What are you people doing in there? Can I come in?"

So the first year Sun Dance started and, well, Barbara's son, Patrick, wanted to dance, you know. He kept asking my daughter, Barbara, "I want to dance. I want to dance beside Grandpa." And, Barbara asked and I said, "He's too young." I said, "Wait 'til you get older." He says, "No, I want to dance beside Grandpa."

So they already started to dance. It was early in the morning they started. So that morning when they first started dancing, I guess.... We always sit in that cookshack. So we were all sitting in there. And, here, Patrick came. He came over and he said, "Did you get my skirt ready? Because I'm going to dance. I'm going to start today." And, here we were all sitting around there just looking at each other. And my mom was sitting there and Ruben's wife, Pansy, and all those old people. So, I said, "No, Patrick, you wait." And, then my mom said, "No, he's a boy. He's a Lakota boy. Make up his own mind. He want to dance, then let him dance." So he was really happy when my mom say that. She said, "I got this skirt for him." We still have that skirt. I don't know where she got it. I don't how she got it. But, she got this little skirt. Just small. A blue one. Yeah, and it had ribbons. She got that from her bag and she said, "I've got a skirt for him."

And, you know, the dancers have eagle feathers. And, Sole and my other granddaughters said, "Oh, boy, Patrick didn't have no eagle fan, so we're going to make one for him." And I was like . . . I thought they were just teasing. At that time, Rae-Ann and Sole was just small girls. So they were really happy that Patrick was going to dance. So they all said, "We're going to help you." So they went in the cookshack and one of Emma Waters's kids brought that turkey, wild turkey. They brought that wild turkey and they were plucking the feathers out. But, they got some feathers and they make a fan in a hurry. And here comes Sole and Rae-Ann and they say, "We make that feather for Patrick. The fan." It was just cute. Patrick was passing by with those turkey feathers and they have a red rag around them and he was really fanning himself!

And, I talked to Earl Swift Hawk, the medicine man. I said, "My grandson wants to come in." I said, "Is it all right?" I told him that he wanted to dance. He told me the same thing. He said, "Good. He's a boy. If he wants to do something then let him." So, I said, "Okay." So I put him out there. And, then my brother's son, Everett, came out right away and in Indian he said, "My cousin, *hanka si*." He said, "My cousin going in?" So, I said, "Yeah." So he came out and they went in the sweat lodge. And I think that was real cute. Two little boys. He was only three and a half.

And when they were resting, I think it was second round, they took Patrick in. He went all around there. And all those people stand up. They were saying, "Everyone stand up, the Sun Dancers are coming in." Everybody was looking and here Patrick was just small, walking in. And everybody say, "What?!?" So he danced. He finished his four days. He finished his four days and he was really strong.

When I first tried to find meaning in Melda's story about her grandson's first Sun Dance, I had focused on the gender issues that are prevalent in the story. In fact, as we saw earlier, I had regarded the entire project along gender lines that differed from Melda and Lupe's conception of the project. Consequently, I interpreted this specific story relating to *women*, in the *cookshack*, *having* to ask a medicine *man* about the commanding decision of a Lakota *boy*. I thought it was about the authority that men have in all spheres of life, specifically the religious and spiritual. In that sense, I missed the point that Melda's mother and the medicine man *corroborated* one another, that traditional authorities were supported in a network of relations. I now understand this story in terms of the changes in Lakota tradition and, more importantly, how to talk about and incorporate those changes.

Melda tells her audience about the constant process of learning from stories and the importance of this practice. For example, in her initial story about her eldest brother, Albert, she says that she regrets not asking more of him. She also indicates that Albert regretted not asking more of his great-grandparents. He says, "I always wonder why." Melda includes these queries in her own account, and we learn about the process of sharing stories. She has fittingly become an expert storyteller herself. She laughs, both quietly and out loud, at many points in her stories, and her tone is overwhelmingly lighthearted. Even when she speaks of hardships, Melda tends to find them heartening and educational, and this comes across in her strength and spirit. In this story about her grandson's first Sun

Dance, Melda recounts the discussion that took place among three generations of women, as well as with the medicine man, in order to determine how to maintain tradition. Melda's enjoyment in telling this story, and her enjoyment in storytelling in general, is integral to the meaning of the story. The *dialogue* that takes place is as significant as her repeated efforts to perpetuate that dialogue. Melda repeatedly uses "she said" and similar phrases to convey the dialogic engagement that is critical to her story. She emphasizes her own learning, achieved through discussion, in coming to understand a traditional practice. In the story, Melda traces *how* an understanding of "tradition" was determined. Her telling of the story promotes a dialogue about traditional practices and, therefore, functions to perpetuate and sustain tradition. The same could be said of the entire project in that Melda and Lupe have recorded their life stories and, in their telling, have perpetuated and sustained Lakota tradition. My own role has been to hear these stories and, appreciating the changes in perspective that they bring, to convey this experience of collaboration to others. In that sense, we have been talking, together, about maintaining all that is related.

Talking Together

In this book, Melda and Lupe have been talking together about their lives. In particular, they have focused on how their lives have intersected with the Lakota spiritual practice of the Sun Dance. Part of what emerges from this discussion is the idea of acknowledging insiders and outsiders in the Lakota community of Pine Ridge Reservation. My own understanding of "insiders" and "outsiders" changed over the course of the project. I found that tradition is, in part, about learning; it is something that is worked on, discussed, and maintained. With this emphasis on learning in a traditional community, everyone is both an insider and outsider as he or she moves through circles of understanding. Concomitantly, I write of my own process in this collaboration—the process of being an outsider who came to know something of what it means to be an insider (Goulet 248). I do this because there is a real need to learn from theoretical perspectives that are derived from culturally based frameworks. Chickasaw educator Eber Hampton provides a telling metaphor for this kind of learning with a story about an elder and his box:

> His question came from behind the box, "How many sides do you see?"
>
> "One," I said.
>
> He pulled the box towards his chest and turned it so one corner faced me. "Now how many do you see?"
>
> "Now I see three sides."
>
> He stepped back and extended the box, one corner towards him and one towards me. "You and I together can see six sides of this box," he told me. (Battiste xvi)

Reevaluating my research practices with Melda and Lupe has required that I recognize and respond to subject positions other than my own; I have had to learn from different perspectives. In *Reclaiming Indigenous Voice and Vision* (2000), Marie Battiste (Mi'kmaq) asserts that "[i]ndigenous knowledge exists and is a legitimate research issue" (xix). Anthropologist Peter Whiteley notes that there is a "marked increase in formal attention to situated perspectives, especially via the influence of Native American critics like Vine Deloria Jr., and Gerald Vizenor, and, more lately, by postcolonial interventions (at least those of metropolitan academics like Spivak, Said, Bhabha, or Trinh)" (16).[1] It is difficult to make generalizations about an ideology that itself contests homogenization, but I suggest that standpoint epistemologies, or situated perspectives, are increasingly prevalent in critical discourse and facilitate new ways of learning.[2] Some examples: Dorothy Smith has made efforts to articulate "a knowledge from our [women's] standpoint . . . situated in the particularities of the local everyday and everynight worlds of our immediate experience" (31). Similarly, Patricia Hill Collins describes "embracing both an Afrocentric worldview and a feminist sensibility and using both to forge a self-defined standpoint" (28). In *Talkin' up to the White Woman: Indigenous Women and Feminism* (2000), Aileen Moreton-Robinson says: "I am representing an Indigenous standpoint within Australian feminism" (xvi).[3] And, speaking cross-culturally, Whiteley describes his process of understanding Hopi discourse and says that Hopi social life involves a relationship between structure and agency that belies the divisions produced by Western epistemological bias (33). These standpoints, perspectives, or "ways of knowing" are rooted in specific cultural traditions and represent ways of understanding the world.

In this project I have followed an introspective, recursive methodology in which early research decisions are analyzed in the light of what I have learned in this apprenticeship in the Lakota community. This model is exemplified in Wendy Wickwire's collaboration with Harry Robinson (Okanagan), *Nature Power: In the Spirit of an Okanagan Storyteller* (1992). Wickwire reflects on being able to write about what she learned from Harry Robinson: "My role has been to help Harry reach a broader audience with his stories. But I am also present as listener and collaborator. I cannot speak for Harry or for the Okanagan people, but I can speak from what I have learned. I was close to Harry; I traveled with him and cared for him. My world and my way of thinking were changed by this experience. Harry knew this" (Robinson, *Nature* 19). My own methodology has been informed by my commitment to being respectful, a value that pervades Lakota social relations, but my understanding of the issues has developed throughout the course of this project.[4] Even during final revisions, I continued to notice times when an analytical tendency might over-write Melda and Lupe's stories or when my own ideas about identity and tradition might overwhelm Melda and Lupe's account. I cannot claim that these sort of academic lapses have been entirely removed; rather, I hope that my intentions, coupled with the textual results, might be instructive. As Judith Butler says, "[t]he point . . . is not then to answer these questions, but to permit them an opening, to provoke a political discourse that sustains the questions" (41).

Finally, in my experiences on the reservation, I learned, among many other things, about the importance of star quilts as critical identity markers in the reservation community and as central to Lakota giveaway ceremonies.[5] A story about quilts therefore bears final mention. The giveaway embodies the ideology of being spiritually wealthy and, correspondingly, materially poor; star quilts are just one of the many important symbols that form a network of meaning in these social circumstances. The star on a star quilt has eight points and is pieced together from many diamond-shaped, multicolored patches. Further reworkings of the star pattern have emerged by juxtaposing a star pattern with Lakota symbols, such as the buffalo, medicine wheel, or eagle.[6] In chapter 3, Melda described learning to quilt as a young girl. Later in her life, her mother had been helping her with a particular quilt, using the "Drunkard's Path" pattern, but Melda ultimately left it unfinished even after her mother's death. She had run out of fabric and was unable to find the same color in local fabric stores. In the meantime, I had taken up quilting with my own mother so that we could make star quilts for giveaways, and we are still quilting all these years later. Melda asked me to find a color match in Vancouver, and she was then able to finish the quilt with the new material. Neither of us, however, would have ever guessed the circumstances under which the quilt would ultimately be finished. Lupe passed away in 1999, and we all felt the loss in his unexpected death. Melda finished her quilt and placed it on Lupe's casket. She honored her husband and her relations in offering a quilt in the traditional manner. Similarly, Melda and Lupe accord honor to their family in telling their life stories. Ultimately, they ensure that tradition is passed on in the most dynamic and essential of ways—their stories pattern a star quilt honoring their relations. In addition, the bringing together of our perspectives resonates as an ongoing enactment of the giveaway exchange.

NOTES

Introduction

1. It is difficult to define Indianness when the vocabulary itself is contested. "Indian," "Native," and "white" all have political connotations. "Lakota"and "Sioux" similarly have a political history in that settlers used "Sioux" to refer to the Lakota people, much like the term "Indian." I have found that "Indian" and "Lakota" are the most common terms in use on Pine Ridge Reservation at present. In accordance with my own habits and in acknowledgment of both Native and non-Native audiences, I use both "Indian" and "Native" but employ the designation "Lakota" rather than "Sioux."

2. In this sense, I follow Helen Hoy's suggestion that identity be treated as a verb, not a noun, to try to gain a better understanding of Indian identity ("Nothing" 177).

3. See Grobsmith for more information on Rosebud Reservation.

4. John Collier repealed anti-religion laws in the 1930s, but there is a continuing history of constraints and legislation. AIM activist Russell Means describes the history of the Sun Dance in his autobiography: "As with many of our spiritual observances, Christian missionaries forced the BIA to ban it [the Sun Dance] in 1881. Our right to the sun dance was restored in the 1950s, but with so many restrictions that the ceremony was reduced to a mere shadow of what it had once been. . . . [But] a few Lakota secretly conducted the holy rituals in remote parts of their reservations" (186). See Holler for a history of the Sun Dance.

5. The American Indian Movement is a pan-Indian national activist organization. See Nagel, Johnson, and Champagne for more information.

6. The interest in Native spirituality in the late 1960s and 1970s, in both Native and non-Native communities, fueled the writing and reissue of several popular books about Lakota culture. *Black Elk Speaks*, the collaborative life story of Nicholas Black Elk, was first published in 1932 and grew in popularity with its reissue in 1961. Reprinted since then, it "continues to have an enduring influence both on and off the reservation" (Bucko 53). Dee Brown's historical account of the Lakota people, *Bury My Heart at Wounded Knee*

(1970), also achieved popular success at that time. Shortly thereafter, Richard Erdoes told the story of John (Fire) Lame Deer in *Lame Deer: Seeker of Visions* (1972). This book, along with many of the other popular Lakota narratives, continues to be used "by many readers as a point of access to and a guide for Lakota ritual practice" (Bucko 72). In the 1970s, Frank Fools Crow, in collaboration with Thomas Mails, also provided well-received narratives about his practices as a medicine man.

7. See Nagel. Dakota scholar Elizabeth Cook-Lynn is clear in differentiating between civil rights and the Native efforts toward self-determination and sovereignty that are associated with being constitutionally recognized nation(s) in the United States. For a further discussion, see Cook-Lynn, *Why* 141.

8. The occupation of Wounded Knee is described in Peter Matthiessen's *In the Spirit of Crazy Horse*; also see Akwesasne Notes's *Voices from Wounded Knee, 1973, in the Words of the Participants.*

1. Impressions

1. Elizabeth Cook-Lynn says, "The Oglala make up one band of the Sioux Nation (the others being Sicangu, Ihanktowan, Sihasapa, Santee, Hunkpapa, and Minneconjou)" (*Anti-Indianism* 22). For further discussion on the meaning of "Sioux," "Lakota," and "Oglala," see Hale 54; Means 209; Heflin 2; Sneve xii; Beatrice Medicine in Harjo and Bird 208; Rice, *Before* 6, 77; and Young Bear and Theisz 18, 84.

2. See Lewis for a history of the district of Allen.

3. I have written this book largely in the present tense, which might raise questions as to whether I am writing in the "ethnographic present" or the "literary present." The ethnographic present functions to convey a "hypothesized pure culture that the ethnographer tries to extract from what are considered the adulterating influences of contact with other, chiefly White, cultures" (Rabillard 5). It is by no means my intention to align myself with such a practice; rather, I want to convey that there are different ways of conceiving of time and, inasmuch as Melda and Lupe's stories enact regeneration as associated with the oral tradition, I feel it best to indicate the ways in which they continue to be active in perpetuating tradition even in my efforts to commit their narrative to the written page.

4. Many ethnographies have been written on some or all of these rites. For Black Elk's description see Joseph Epes Brown's *The Sacred Pipe*. Julian

Rice provides one of the most recent comprehensive analyses of Lakota belief and ritual in *Before the Great Spirit*. Many other prominent Dakota and Lakota ethnographies were written in the late 1800s and early 1900s. See, for example, Lynd; G. H. Pond; S. W. Pond; Fletcher; Riggs; Dorsey; Mooney; Walker, *Lakota Belief*, *Lakota Myth*, and *Lakota Society*; Wissler; Eastman; Densmore; Bushotter; Buechel; and E. Deloria, *Dakota Texts*, *Speaking of Indians*, and *Waterlily*. Of Walker's ethnographic work, Rice says: "Three recent additions of his papers, *Lakota Belief and Ritual* (1980), *Lakota Society* (1982), and *Lakota Myth* (1983) have become a compendium of tribal truth for both New Age entrepreneurs and serious scholars" (*Before* 10). Severt Young Bear also notes their usefulness to the Lakota people (Young Bear and Theisz 99).

5. The *yuwipi* ceremony is a "Lakota ritual in which the holy man is bound in a darkened room and obtains release through the mysterious intercession of helping spirits. Employed in contemporary times for spiritual devotion and to find lost objects" (Holler 230).

6. For a description of the four directions, see Arlene Fire's (Dakota) account in Harjo and Bird 303.

7. See Ellis for further information on the history of powwows.

8. Speaking of her grandmother's life story, Dakota historian Angela Cavendar Wilson says that this "account by itself will not change the course of American history, or create a theory or framework. . . . It is not even representative of the 'Dakota perspective.' Instead, it is one family's perspective that in combination with other families' stories might help to create an understanding of Dakota views on [a specific] event and time period" (12).

4. Collaboration

1. See, for example, Devon A. Mihesuah's edited collection, *Natives and Academics: Researching and Writing about American Indians*. The essays were originally published in *American Indian Quarterly* 20.1 (1996).

2. To this point, Jace Weaver asks: "who is 'enriched' and who diminished?" (228).

3. One of the first outcries around effective representation followed from the publication, in 1979, of Ruth Beebe Hill's popular *Hanta Yo: An American Saga*. This heavily criticized story was a fictional portrayal of the Sioux in the 1800s. Dakota scholar Elizabeth Cook-Lynn notes that "[t]he Sioux considered the novel's depiction of their lives and histories false and obscene,

and surprisingly, they began to say so publicly—in the media, in academia, and everywhere in between" (*Why* 65).

4. Representing the words of Native storytellers is also the subject of ethnopoetics, whereby textual strategies have been suggested to better convey the oral quality of the work. See Tedlock; Hymes; Dauenhauer and Dauenhauer; Kroeber; and Toelken.

5. See McCluskey. In the 1990s the Black Elk material became implicated in questions about the invention of tradition. Alan Hanson says, "invention is an ordinary event in the development of all discourse" (899). Jocelyn Linnekin further elaborates that "[s]ymbolically constructed traditions are therefore not inauthentic; rather, all traditions—Western and indigenous—are invented, in that they are symbolically constructed in the present and reflect contemporary concerns and purposes rather than a passively inherited legacy" (447). For the more recent concerns over the Black Elk material, see, for example, Powers, "When Black Elk Speaks, Everybody Listens."

6. See, for example, V. Deloria, *Sender*; and DeMallie, *Sixth*.

7. *Lakota Woman* was first published in 1990, although it was completed in 1979. *Ohitika Woman* followed in 1994. Mary Brave Woman is now divorced from Leonard Crow Dog, and she has used several different names. See Petrillo.

8. Arnold Krupat excludes the books from his anthology of Native American literature because of Richard Erdoes's involvement. See Krupat, *Native American Autobiography.*

9. In using this practice I have been influenced primarily by the following ethnographies: Cruikshank et al.; Whiteley; Goulet; and Spielmann. For a description of this ethnographic method in the study of Native cultures specifically, see Krupat, *Ethnocriticism*; and Lassiter.

10. Wendy Wickwire's collaboration with Harry Robinson (Okanagan) is one obvious exception to cautions about cross-gender fieldwork. See Robinson, *Nature Power* and *Write It on Your Heart.*

6. Affiliation: Lupe

1. Spivak defines the subaltern as "persons with little access to social mobility" (Spivak et al. 218).

2. Following John Beverley's usage, I take "us" to mean academics concerned about representing the subaltern (1). In this case, the "we versus

them" dynamic is important given the ways the discussion of the subaltern itself maintains that division.

3. The dialogue in this chapter also shows how our open-ended discussions have, at times, been edited to read as more sustained narratives.

4. Collectivity is maintained through "the oppositional process by which difference and boundary are maintained" (Cruikshank, *Social* 43). By strategically using culture, marginalized groups undermine the presumed non-Native norm of being "without culture." As anthropologist Marshall Sahlins says: "The cultural self-consciousness developing among imperialism's erstwhile victims is one of the more remarkable phenomena of world history in the later twentieth century. 'Culture'—the word itself, or some local equivalent, is on everyone's lips. Tibetans and Hawaiians, Ojibway, Kwakiutl, and Eskimo, Kasakhs and Mongols, native Australians, Balinese, Kashmiris, and New Zealand Maori: all discover they have a 'culture.' For centuries they may have hardly noticed it. But now, as the New Guinean said to the anthropologist, 'If we didn't have *kastom* [customs], we would be just like white men'" (3).

5. According to the 1995 Comisión Nacional del Agua, the population of Silao, Guanajuato, is 51,596 (Pablos).

6. See, for example, this account in Bucko: "Eagles came to the ceremony. They said they know my problem. They understood, and they'll help me. I went to the lake and looked to the west. Some thunder beings were coming up and there was a red cloud above and gray and white—black and red came together. A voice said when the black and red come together, you'll never drink again. They came together. I watched. I had an uplifting feeling" (172).

7. "The 'Red Road' . . . signifies the good, traditional Lakota way. To the Lakota the medicine wheel . . . is a symbol of cosmos. The direction ('road') south-north is the red road which stands for harmony and life, whereas the direction ('road') east-west symbolizes warfare and destruction" (Kurkiala 214).

8. See Duran and Duran for a discussion of the interconnections between colonialism and alcoholism. Internalized oppression occurs when "people have turned their rage inward" (Rice, *Before* 4). In *Before the Great Spirit: The Many Faces of Sioux Spirituality* (1998), Julian Rice uses Lakota cosmology to describe the reclaiming of strength and identity. The Thunders are spiritual

beings associated with protection and destruction. According to Rice, they play a role in resistance and recovery as well as in despair and dislocation: "life seems completely out of control, as if the Thunders that were once their friends now threaten to break them apart. The narrators counsel a return to spiritual practices that would once again make the Thunders their primary protectors. The forces that have caused so many Lakota to destroy themselves in alcohol or intratribal violence can become the forces that bring new life, when traditional priorities in prayer are remembered" (98).

8. Generation: Melda

1. See Irwin for further information on legislation around religious freedom in the United States.

2. In the *yuwipwi* ceremony, a "medicine man, wrapped in a robe and securely tied with thongs, is released mysteriously by spirit helpers . . . [who] give messages concerning future events, cures, and lost objects" (DeMallie, *Sixth* 13).

3. Leonard Crow Dog says, "The dog is sacred. . . . Every once in a while the dog will bark toward the east and the west. When somebody dies he'll be calling to the family, barking. The dog sees the spirits, the dead souls. The dog knows when someone is about to die, but you don't know it" (L. Crow Dog and Erdoes 124). Lakota writer and educator Delphine Red Shirt further describes the respect and honor associated with the *yuwipi* ceremony: "Our *yuwipi* ceremonies are when we come together and lose track of time in song and prayer. It is a period when we enter the womb of time and emerge on the other side whole and happy, like we used to be. . . . When the ceremony is over, we say '*Mitakuye oyas'i*,' meaning 'My relatives, I pray for; all of them, I pray for'" (*Bead* 111).

4. Delphine Red Shirt says, "A grandparent is revered and loved. If a person lives to see two generations, he or she deserves respect. If a person lives to see three or perhaps four generations, he or she is considered sacred" (*Turtle* 73).

5. Bruce Miller explains how kinship ties facilitate an authoritative role within Native communities: "At both private and public gatherings, the moral basis for the legitimacy of the grandmothers' 'teachings' is derived in part from age and experience but also from kinship ties and biological links to the audience. These kinship ties are commonly made explicit through

recitations of genealogy or through commentary about the interrelatedness of the tribal members" (111).

6. Guy Gibbon describes the *tiyospaye* structure: "Lakota loyalties moved outward from the family to the nation in a series of concentric circles. In the innermost circle was the family, which was composed of one or more tipi households, for polygynous marriage, where a man has more than one wife simultaneously, was an accepted practice among the Sioux before the reservation period. A camp was composed of two or more husbanded tipi households, and one or more camps formed a band (a *tiospaye*). . . . A group of related bands formed a tribe, such as the Oglala, and groups of related tribes formed a division of the Sioux Nation, here the Lakota" (101).

7. See also E. Deloria's *Speaking of Indians* and *Waterlily.*

10. Identity

1. The most extensive account of the *hunka* ceremony is in Black Elk's *The Sacred Pipe*, 101–15. Kenneth Lincoln elaborates that "an adoption is a spiritual tie. . . . It involves extended kinship into the Sioux community and culture" (738). In *Choteau Creek: A Sioux Reminiscence* (1992), Joseph Iron Eye Dudley says that "in Sioux culture there are claimed relatives, what sociologists call fictive kin. They are relatives in a cultural and social sense, but not biologically or legally. It is a kinship that is beyond even the extended family. . . . It is a claimed relationship" (121).

2. See Rose. See also E. Deloria's *Speaking of Indians* for a discussion of outmarriage practices.

3. According to the 2000 census, the reservation's Mexican population is estimated at 140 (0.9%) and the white population at 969 (6.2%).

4. The pipe was brought to the Lakota people by the White Buffalo Calf Woman. For the myth of the White Buffalo Calf Woman see Powers, *Oglala Religion*, 82–83. Gibbon discusses the history of the pipe and says that "the 'coming of the pipe,' if it was rooted in an actual historical event, occurred sometime after [c. AD 1300]; counting backward through the recorded number of the 'keepers of the pipe' puts this event near the beginning of the nineteenth century" (240 n. 45). The original pipe is kept at Green Grass, and a medicine man is designated as the keeper of the pipe. In many ways, Green Grass can be regarded as "the religious center of the Sioux world" (Steinmetz 16).

5. Cook-Lynn notes that "[t]he interest in decolonization goes back to the

Mayan resistance narratives of the 1500s and has always played an important role in political and social life" (*Why* 96).

6. Vickers elaborates on the ramifications of blood-quantum arguments: "racial criteria have had and continue to have a destabilizing and de-racinating effect on Indian identities, confounding any meaningful discussion of 'Indianness,' a concept that grows less and less definitive, as perhaps it must, as time and this discussion go on. As historian Limerick has explained, 'Set the blood quantum at one-quarter, hold to it as a rigid definition of Indians, let intermarriage proceed as it has for centuries, and eventually Indians will be defined out of existence.'. . . Thus the blood quantum argument is a major conundrum that vexes Indian identity at its very core" (164).

7. Please note that the usage of *race* in this book is meant to convey "race" as a socially constructed concept. The association of blood quantum, heredity, and visible difference are all important to "racial" constructions of Indian identity.

12. Tradition

1. Quanah Parker (Comanche), an Oklahoma peyotist, helped to bring the Half Moon style of peyote meetings to other tribes. The Cross Fire branch also developed later.

2. The Lakotas regard the Black Hills as sacred, and Harney Peak has been a location of both prayer and protest. The Black Hills area is perhaps best known as the site of Mount Rushmore. Treaty negotiations continue to take place frequently concerning the Black Hills. Ownership of the land was among the grievances during the siege at Wounded Knee in 1973. Paul Robertson explains the issues, which continue today, in *The Power of the Land: Identity, Ethnicity, and Class among the Oglala Lakota* (2002). He says: "The 1869 Fort Laramie Treaty established boundaries for the Great Sioux Reservation and stipulated that the U.S. would provide rations, annuity payments, and cattle. The U.S. also agreed to use its military power to prevent entry of non-Indians into the Black Hills. . . . The theft of 7.7 million acres of land was given a legal veneer by the so-called 'Agreement of 1876,' which was passed by the U.S. Congress as the Black Hills Act of 1877. The Act contravened Article 12 of the 1868 Fort Laramie Treaty, which provides that ¾ of the signatures of all of the adult males were requisite to any land cessions, and was fully ruled as an illegal taking by the U.S. Supreme Court in 1980" (20).

3. For a discussion of the interrelations among land, culture, and economy see Pickering, *Lakota Culture*; and Robertson.

4. *Wasicu* might have originally meant "'white' or 'snow' of the north, *Waziya*" and been associated with sacred beings (Lincoln and Slagle 104). It can also mean "many" and refer to settlers (Black Elk DeSersa et al. 5). See also E. Deloria's *Speaking of Indians*.

5. See Mooney for a further description. See Coleman for a timeline and history.

6. On December 29, 1890, three hundred unarmed men, women, and children were killed by U.S. soldiers at Wounded Knee Creek. The site of the massacre was later occupied in 1973 by AIM members and Lakota traditionalists in an effort to grieve unjust conditions on the reservation.

7. For a fuller account of the story Melda relates about the healing effects of the Ghost Dance, see L. Crow Dog and Erdoes 43. The account is attributed to Howard Red Bear, Melda's great-uncle.

8. Bucko gives an account of a Lakota man describing the races as associated with the colors of the cardinal directions: "The four colors [red, yellow, white, black] represent the four races. So you can't discriminate. Some say just Indians, no *ska wichasa* ['white people']. Then they say *mitakuye iyuha* 'all my relative.' To me they [the colors associated with the cardinal directions] represent the four races" (198).

9. In 1993, Lakota spiritual and political leaders passed the "Declaration of War Against Exploiters of Lakota Spirituality," which was brought to the attention of the United Nations (Fenelon 295). The Sun Dance controversy proliferated in 1997 with several articles in the national Indian newspaper *Indian Country Today*, which listed medicine men accused of selling the Sun Dance to non-Native participants (see, e.g., Porterfield).

10. This refers to a song from the sweat lodge ceremony (*inipi*).

11. The account recorded in William Powers's *Yuwipi* also shows this connection between "sending a voice" and prayer: "I send a voice above. With the pipe, I send a voice above. 'I do this because I want to live with my relations.' Saying this over and over, I pray to *Tunkasila*" (43). Delphine Red Shirt explains: "'*Wachékiye*,' she prays. The word '*waché*,' meaning 'I cry,' and '*kiyá*,' meaning 'to send out.' . . . She sent forth her voice, her cry, her plea to be heard. Her voice was the vehicle for redemption. . . . In Lakota, there was no such thing as silent prayer, it had to be spoken, to be heard. It

had to be sent out. It came from a silent place within. It became a cry sent out, in a single heartbeat, it emerged, it went forth" (*Turtle* 64).

14. Knowledge

1. Research in the humanities and social sciences is often subsumed under protocols that dictate scientific procedures. In the United States, research is governed by the National Institutes of Health (NIH), whose guidelines are, in turn, upheld by institutional review boards (IRBs). In Canada, the Social Sciences and Humanities Research Council of Canada (SSHRC), the National Sciences and Engineering Research Council (NSERC), and the Canadian Institutes of Health Research (CIHR) have issued the "Tri-Council Policy Statement: Ethical Conduct for Research Involving Humans." For a further discussion of the incompatibility of social science research and scientific ethics procedures see "Protecting Human Beings: Institutional Review Boards and Social Science Research." Also, the Oral History Association has issued a policy statement regarding oral history research and IRB oversight (see "An Update: Excluding Oral History from IRB Review"). Robert B. Townsend and Meriam Belli of the American Historical Association write of these issues in the spring 2005 *Oral History Association Newsletter.*

2. The specific legitimating bodies associated with Pine Ridge Reservation conceivably authorize projects in ways that differ from those employed by other nations and by academic and governing institutions. Recent Lakota ethnographies, autobiographies, and collaborations do not address Lakota tribal council protocols. The Native American Research Guidelines Advisory Committee (NARGAC), formed at Northern Arizona University in 1991, deals with some of the issues raised by complex tribal organization. Information on NARGAC comes from an April 1994 Anthro-L posting that contains information from anthropologist Deward E. Walker Jr. and Choctaw scholar Devon A. Mihesuah ("Native"). The members of NARGAC are cited as Devon A. Mihesuah, Nicholas J. Meyerhofer, Shirley Powell, Robert T. Trotter II, and Peter L. van der Loo. They urge that the tribe should be represented by "the Native elected representatives, elders, and/or traditional leaders of the community." The committee recognizes that "the tribe may be divided along political, social, religious, geographic or class lines," but there is little consensus as to what should be done in the event that there is a division between the "tribes' elected political and religious leadership." Recognizing an imminent deadlock, Mihesuah suggests that "[n]o single set of guide-

lines will work in all situations." She recognizes that tribes differ in their approaches and recommends that "respect, dialogue, and compromise" guide research practices.

3. Severt Young Bear indicates that having fifteen to twenty thousand people under one tribal leadership is difficult. He notes that the district council in Porcupine has twenty-four hundred members, which is "too many," especially as contrasted with the traditional structure of the *tiyospaye* (Young Bear and Theisz 118).

4. The issue of disclosing spiritual practices is even debated among Native writers. For example, Paula Gunn Allen (Laguna) has described her uneasiness in teaching aspects of Leslie Marmon Silko's (Laguna) *Ceremony*, since it makes ceremony public. See Allen; and Silko, *Conversations*.

5. On June 25, 1876, General George Armstrong Custer and his entire command were defeated by Lakota and Cheyenne warriors in the famous Battle of Little Bighorn. On December 29, 1890, the Seventh Cavalry killed three hundred Indians, many of them women and children, in the massacre at Wounded Knee. Wounded Knee is emblematic of the struggles that have taken place over the course of colonial and settler history.

6. According to George Kills in Sight (Lakota), Crazy Horse's father had those at the grave site smoke a pipe and pledge that they would not reveal the location of the grave (Cash and Hoover 64). In his autobiography, Russell Means (Lakota) states, "[a]ccording to one story, Crazy Horse's bones and heart are buried at Wounded Knee" (290). Mario Gonzalez (Lakota) and Elizabeth Cook-Lynn provide the following account in reference to Crazy Horse's burial place: "When they got to talking about the burial place of Crazy Horse, a bit of silence fell upon the group. Mario had told them he had always heard stories about Crazy Horse being buried in the Manderson–Wounded Knee area but he was told by Robert Dillon, a son of Emily Standing Bear-Dillon, that his remains were moved several times and the final burial site is east of Wanblee" (189).

Conclusion

1. Using Ato Quayson's definition of *postcolonialism* as "a studied engagement with the experience of colonialism and its past and present effects" (2), I follow his suggestion that "postmodernism can never fully explain the state of the contemporary world without first becoming postcolonial, and vice versa" (154).

2. In *Decolonizing Methodologies* (1999), Linda Tuhiwai Smith talks about an "indigenous language of critique" and a "local theoretical positioning" from her perspective as a Maori researcher. She describes a Kaupapa Maori "way of looking at the world" as involving a Maori "epistemological tradition which frames the way we see the world, the way we organize ourselves in it, the questions we ask and the solution which we seek" (187). As such, her assertion can be seen as part of a larger postcolonial effort to reposition knowledges from specific perspectives.

3. Tuhiwai Smith elaborates on Native North American political stances: "The concept of indigenist, says Ward Churchill, means 'that I am one who not only takes the rights of indigenous peoples as the highest priority of my political life, but who draws upon the traditions—the bodies of knowledge and corresponding codes of values.' . . . M. Annette Jaimes refers to indigenism as being grounded in the alternative conceptions of world view and value systems" (146).

4. Kurkiala notes that "Lakota often emphasize 'respect' as their primary social value" (173).

5. "Community giveaways are held for several reasons: as part of annual powwows, to commemorate graduations, as memorials for departed loved ones, as part of naming and *huká* [*hunka*], or adoption, ceremonies, and in conjunction with other events that involve honoring an individual or group. . . . During these occasions, the sponsoring family distributes objects . . . [generating an] obligation of long-term generalized reciprocity" (Pickering, *Lakota Culture* 57).

6. Quilting is a relatively recent practice in reservation communities. Patricia Albers states that "[t]he art of quiltmaking has been practiced by Sioux women for nearly a century. It was introduced to them through government and church agencies" ("Role" 126). She says, "the star quilt has come to represent the preservation of family and community honor . . . [quilts have] achieved the status of an ethnic banner, upholding all of those meanings and symbols that signify Sioux traditionalism" (133). Star quilts are "one of the most prestigious items in the Sioux giveaway system. They are given at memorial feasts, naming ceremonies, homecoming celebrations for veterans, and in the 'donations' of powwow officials. When given away for honorific purposes, star quilts bestow respect on both the giver and receiver" (131). The star pattern is connected to the Star of Bethlehem or the Lone Star pattern

that is found in non-Native quilting traditions. But, Albers also suggests that Lakota women configured the pattern from ceremonial hide robes, which had a traditional morning star design (124). She says: "The morning star, which appears in the East in early April . . . represents the direction from which spirits of the dead travel to earth, and by extension, it signifies a continuing link between the living and the dead" (129).

Akwesasne Notes. *Voices from Wounded Knee, 1973, in the Words of the Participants.* Rooseveltown NY: Akwesasne Notes, 1974.

Albers, Patricia. "The Role of Sioux Women in the Production of Ceremonial Objects: The Case of the Star Quilt." *The Hidden Half: Studies of Plains Indian Women.* Ed. Patricia Albers and Beatrice Medicine. Lanham MD: UP of America, 1983. 123–40.

———. "Sioux Women in Transition: A Study of Their Changing Status in Domestic and Capitalist Sectors of Production." *The Hidden Half: Studies of Plains Indian Women.* Ed. Patricia Albers and Beatrice Medicine. Lanham MD: UP of America, 1983. 175–234.

Allen, Paula Gunn. "Special Problems in Teaching Leslie Marmon Silko's *Ceremony.*" *Leslie Marmon Silko's Ceremony: A Casebook.* Ed. Allan Chavkin. Oxford: Oxford UP, 2002. 83–90.

Battiste, Marie. "Introduction: Unfolding the Lessons of Colonization." *Reclaiming Indigenous Voice and Vision.* Ed. Marie Battiste. Vancouver: U of British Columbia P, 2000. xvi–xxx.

Beverley, John. *Subalternity and Representation: Arguments in Cultural Theory.* Durham NC: Duke UP, 1999.

Black Elk DeSersa, Esther, Olivia Black Elk Pourier, Aaron DeSersa Jr., and Clifton DeSersa. *Black Elk Lives: Conversations with the Black Elk Family.* Ed. Hilda Neihardt and Lori Utecht. Lincoln: U of Nebraska P, 2000.

Brave Bird, Mary, and Richard Erdoes. *Ohitika Woman.* New York: HarperPerennial, 1994.

Brown, Dee. *Bury My Heart at Wounded Knee.* New York: Holt, Rinehart, and Winston, 1970.

Brown, Joseph Epes. *The Sacred Pipe: Black Elk's Account of the Seven Rites of the Oglala Sioux.* Norman: U of Oklahoma P, 1953.

Bucko, Raymond A. *The Lakota Ritual of the Sweat Lodge: History and Contemporary Practice.* Lincoln: U of Nebraska P, 1998.

Buechel, Eugene. *A Grammar of Lakota.* St. Francis SD: Rosebud Educational Society, 1939.

Bushotter, George. *Teton Myths*. Ed. and trans. Ella Deloria. Boas Collection 30. Philadelphia: American Philosophical Society, 1937.

Cash, Joseph H., and Herbert T. Hoover, eds. *To Be an Indian: An Oral History*. New York: Holt, Rinehart and Winston, 1971.

Coleman, William S. E. *Voices of Wounded Knee*. Lincoln: U of Nebraska P, 2000.

Collins, Patricia Hill. *Black Feminist Thought: Knowledge, Consciousness, and the Politics of Empowerment*. Boston: Unwin Hyman, 1990.

Cook-Lynn, Elizabeth. *Anti-Indianism in Modern America: A Voice from Tatekeya's Earth*. Urbana: U of Illinois P, 2001.

———. "How Scholarship Defames the Native Voice . . . and Why." *Wicazo Sa Review* 15.2 (2000): 79–92.

———. *Why I Can't Read Wallace Stegner and Other Essays: A Tribal Voice*. Madison: U of Wisconsin P, 1996.

Crow Dog, Leonard, and Richard Erdoes. *Crow Dog: Four Generations of Sioux Medicine Men*. New York: HarperCollins, 1995.

Crow Dog, Mary, and Richard Erdoes. *Lakota Woman*. New York: HarperPerennial, 1991.

Cruikshank, Julie. *The Social Life of Stories: Narrative and Knowledge in the Yukon Territory*. Vancouver: U of British Columbia P, 1998.

Cruikshank, Julie, Angela Sidney, Kitty Smith, and Annie Ned. *Life Lived Like a Story: Life Stories of Three Yukon Native Elders*. Lincoln: U of Nebraska P, 1990.

Dauenhauer, Nora Marks, and Richard Dauenhauer. *Haa Shuka/Our Ancestors: Tlingit Oral Narratives*. Seattle: U of Washington P, 1987.

De Leon, Armoldo. "Region and Ethnicity: Topographical Identities in Texas." *Many Wests: Place, Culture and Regional Identity*. Ed. David M. Wrobel and Michael C. Steiner. Lawrence: U of Kansas P, 1997. 259–74.

Deloria, Ella. *Dakota Texts*. 1932. New York: AMS, 1974.

———. *Speaking of Indians*. Vermillion SD: Dakota Press, 1979.

———. *Waterlily*. Lincoln: U of Nebraska P, 1988.

Deloria, Vine, Jr. *Custer Died for Your Sins: An Indian Manifesto*. New York: Avon, 1969.

———. *For This Land: Writings on Religion in America*. Ed. James Treat. New York: Routledge, 1999.

———. Introduction. *Black Elk Speaks*. Lincoln: U of Nebraska P, 1979. xi–xiv.

————, ed. *A Sender of Words: Essays in Memory of John G. Neihardt*. Salt Lake City: Howe Brothers, 1984.

DeMallie, Raymond J. "John G. Neihardt's Lakota Legacy." *A Sender of Words: Essays in Memory of John G. Neihardt*. Ed. Vine Deloria Jr. Salt Lake City: Howe Brothers, 1984. 110–34.

————. "Lakota Traditionalism: History and Symbol." *Native North American Interaction Patterns*. Ed. Regna Darnell and Michael K. Foster. Hull, Quebec: Canadian Museum of Civilization, 1988. 2–21.

————. *The Sixth Grandfather: Black Elk's Teaching Given to John G. Neihardt*. Lincoln: U of Nebraska P, 1984.

DeMallie, Raymond J., and Douglas R. Parks. Introduction. *Sioux Indian Religion: Tradition and Innovation*. Ed. Raymond J. DeMallie and Douglas R. Parks. Norman: U of Oklahoma P, 1987. 3–22.

Densmore, Frances. *Teton Sioux Music*. Smithsonian Institution Bureau of Ethnology Bulletin 61. Washington DC: Government Printing Office, 1918.

Dorsey, James. *A Study of Siouan Cults*. 1894. Seattle: Shorey, 1972.

Dudley, Joseph Iron Eye. *Choteau Creek: A Sioux Reminiscence*. Lincoln: U of Nebraska P, 1992.

Duran, Eduardo, and Bonnie Duran. *Native American Postcolonial Psychology*. Albany: State U of New York P, 1995.

Eastman, Charles A. *Indian Boyhood*. New York: McClure, 1902.

Edelstein, Marilyn. "Resisting Postmodernism; or, 'A Postmodernism of Resistance': bell hooks and the Theory Debates." *Other Sisterhoods: Literary Theory and U.S. Women of Color*. Ed Sandra Kumanato Stanley. Chicago U of Illinois P, 1998. 86–118.

Ellis, Clyde. *A Dancing People: Powwow Culture on the Southern Plains*. Lawrence: UP of Kansas, 2003.

Federal Emergency Management Agency. 2004. Region VIII. 9 June 2005 <http://www.fema.gov/regions/viii/tribal/oglalabg.shtm>.

Fenelon, James V. *Culturcide, Resistance, and Survival of the Lakota ("Sioux Nation")*. New York: Garland, 1998.

Fletcher, Alice. "Indian Ceremonies." *Report of the Peabody Museum of American Archaeology and Ethnology* 16 (1884): 260–333.

Gardner, Susan. "Speaking of Ella Deloria: Conversations with Joyzelle Gingway Godfrey, 1998–2000, Lower Brule Community College, South Dakota." *American Indian Quarterly* 24.3 (2000): 456–81.

Gibbon, Guy. *The Sioux: The Dakota and Lakota Nations.* Malden MA: Blackwell, 2003.

Giltrow, Janet. *Academic Writing: Writing and Reading across Disciplines.* 2nd ed. Peterborough ON: Broadview, 1999.

Gonzalez, Mario, and Elizabeth Cook-Lynn. *The Politics of Hallowed Ground: Wounded Knee and the Struggle for Indian Sovereignty.* Urbana: U of Illinois P, 1999.

Goulet, Jean-Guy A. *Ways of Knowing: Experience, Knowledge, and Power among the Dene Tha.* Vancouver: U of British Columbia P, 1998.

Grobsmith, Elizabeth S. *Lakota of the Rosebud: A Contemporary Ethnography.* New York: Holt, Rinehart, and Winston, 1981.

Hale, Janet Campbell. *Bloodlines: Odyssey of a Native Daughter.* New York: Harper, 1993.

Hanson, Allan. "The Making of the Maori: Culture Invention and Its Logic." *American Anthropologist* 91 (1989): 890–902.

Harjo, Joy, and Gloria Bird. *Reinventing the Enemy's Language: Contemporary Native Women's Writings of North America.* New York: Norton, 1997.

Heflin, Ruth J. "Examples for the World: Four Transitional Sioux Writers and the Sioux Literary Renaissance." Diss. Oklahoma State University, 1997.

Hill, Ruth Beebe. *Hanta Yo: An American Saga.* New York: Warner, 1979.

Holler, Clyde. *Black Elk's Religion: The Sun Dance and Lakota Catholicism.* Syracuse NY: Syracuse UP, 1995.

Hoy, Helen. "'Nothing But the Truth': Discursive Transparency in Beatrice Culleton." *Ariel: A Review of International English Literature* 25.1 (1994): 155–84.

———. "'When You Admit You're a Thief, Then You Can Be Honorable': Native/Non-Native Collaboration in 'The Book of Jessica.'" *Canadian Literature* 136 (1993): 24–39.

Hymes, Dell. *"In Vain I Tried to Tell You": Essays in Native American Ethnopoetics.* Philadelphia: U of Pennsylvania P, 1981.

Irwin, Lee. "Freedom, Law, and Prophecy: A Brief History of Native American Religious Resistance." *Native American Spirituality: A Critical Reader.* Ed. L. Irwin. Lincoln: U of Nebraska P, 2000. 295–316.

Kadlecek, Edward, and Mabell Kadlecek. *To Kill an Eagle: Indian Views on the Last Days of Crazy Horse.* Boulder: Johnson, 1981.

Katz, Jane, ed. *Messengers of the Wind*. New York: Ballantine, 1995.

King, Thomas. "Godzilla vs. Post-Colonial." *World Literature Written in English* 30.2 (1990): 10–16.

Kroeber, Karl. *Retelling/Rereading: The Fate of Storytelling in Modern Times*. New Brunswick NJ: Rutgers UP, 1992.

Krupat, Arnold. *Ethnocriticism: Ethnography, History, Literature*. Berkeley: U of California P, 1992.

———, ed. *Native American Autobiography: An Anthology*. Madison: U of Wisconsin P, 1994.

Kurkiala, Mikael. *"Building the Nation Back Up": The Politics of Identity on the Pine Ridge Indian Reservation*. Uppsala Studies in Cultural Anthropology 22. Uppsala, Sweden: Acta Universitatis Upsaliensis, 1997.

Lame Deer, John Fire, and Richard Erdoes. *Lame Deer: Seeker of Visions*. New York: Washington Square P, 1972.

Lassiter, Luke Eric. "Commentary: Authoritative Texts, Collaborative Ethnography, and Native American Studies." *American Indian Quarterly* 24.4 (2001): 601–14.

Lewis, Emily H. *Wo'Wakita: Reservation Recollections: A People's History of the Allen Issue Station District on the Pine Ridge Indian Reservation of South Dakota*. Sioux Falls SD: Center for Western Studies, 1980.

Lincoln, Kenneth. *Men Down West*. Santa Barbara: Capra, 1997.

Lincoln, Kenneth, with Al Logan Slagle. *The Good Red Road: Passages into Native America*. San Francisco: Harper and Row, 1987.

Linnekin, Jocelyn. "Cultural Invention and the Dilemma of Authenticity." *American Anthropologist* 93 (1991): 446–49.

Lionnet, Françoise. *Postcolonial Representations: Women, Literature, Identity*. Ithaca: Cornell UP, 1995.

Little Bear, Leroy. "Jagged Worldviews Colliding." *Reclaiming Indigenous Voice and Vision*. Ed. Marie Battiste. Vancouver: U of British Columbia P, 2000. 77–85.

Lynd, James W. "The Religion of the Dakotas." *Minnesota Historical Collections* 2 (1864): 150–74.

Mails, Thomas, and Frank Fools Crow. *Fools Crow*. Garden City NY: Doubleday, 1979.

Matthiessen, Peter. *In the Spirit of Crazy Horse*. New York: Viking, 1983.

McCluskey, Sally. "Black Elk Speaks and So Does John Neihardt." *Western American Literature* 4 (1972): 231–42.

Means, Russell. *Where White Men Fear to Tread: The Autobiography of Russell Means*. New York: St. Martin's, 1995.

Medicine, Beatrice. "The Anthropologist and American Indian Studies." *The American Indian Reader: Anthropology*. Ed. Jeannette Henry. San Francisco: Indian Historian, 1972. 13–20.

Mihesuah, Devon A., ed. *Natives and Academics: Researching and Writing about American Indians*. Lincoln: U of Nebraska P, 1998.

Miller, Bruce G. "Discontinuities in the Statuses of Puget Sound Grandmothers." *American Indian Grandmothers: Traditions and Transitions*. Ed. Marjorie M. Schweitzer. Albuquerque: U of New Mexico P, 1999. 104–24.

Mooney, James. *The Ghost-Dance Religion and the Sioux Outbreak of 1890*. Chicago, 1896.

Moreton-Robinson, Aileen. *Talkin' up to the White Woman: Indigenous Women and Feminism*. St. Lucia, Queensland: U of Queensland P, 2000.

Nagel, Joane. *American Indian Ethnic Renewal: Red Power and the Resurgence of Identity and Culture*. New York: Oxford UP, 1996.

Nagel, Joane, Troy Johnson, and Duane Champagne, eds. *American Indian Activism: Alcatraz to the Longest Walk*. Chicago: U of Illinois P, 1997

"Native American Research." Online posting. 1 Apr. 1994. Anthro-L. 23 June 2004 <http://listserv.acsu.buffalo.edu/cgi-bin/wa?A2=ind9404&L=anthro-l&F=&S=&P=751>.

Neihardt, John G. *Black Elk Speaks*. 1932. Lincoln: U of Nebraska P, 1961.

Pablos, Nicolás Pineda. "Urban Water Policy in Mexico: Municipalization and Privatization of Water Services." Diss. U of Texas at Austin, 1999. School of Sonant [*El Colegio de Sonora*]. 9 June 2005 <http://www.colson.edu.mx/Estudios%20Pol/Tesis/cap5.htm>.

Paine, Robert. "Aboriginality, Authenticity, and the Settler World." *Signifying Identities: Anthropological Perspectives on Boundaries and Contested Values*. Ed. Anthony P. Cohen. London: Routledge, 2000. 77–116.

Peltier, Leonard. *Prison Writings*. New York: St. Martin's, 1999.

Petrillo, Larissa. "The Life Stories of a Woman from Rosebud: Names and Naming in *Lakota Woman* and *Ohitika Woman*." MA thesis, Wilfrid Laurier University, 1996.

Pickering, Kathleen. *Lakota Culture, World Economy.* Lincoln: U of Nebraska P, 2000.

———. Rev. of Raymond Bucko's *The Lakota Ritual of the Sweat Lodge.* *American Indian Quarterly* 23.3–4 (1999): 185–87.

Pond, Gideon H. "Dakota Superstitions." *Minnesota Historical Society* 2 (1867): 32–62.

Pond, Samuel W. *The Dakota or Sioux in Minnesota As They Were in 1834.* 1908. St. Paul: Minnesota Historical P, 1986.

Porterfield, K. Marie. "The Selling of the Sun Dance." *Indian Country Today* 28 July 1997: A1+.

Powers, William K. *Oglala Religion.* Lincoln: U of Nebraska P, 1977.

———. "When Black Elk Speaks, Everybody Listens." *Religion in Native North America.* Ed. C. Vecsey. Moscow ID: U of Idaho P, 1990. 136–51.

———. *Yuwipi.* Lincoln: U of Nebraska P, 1982.

"Protecting Human Beings: Institutional Review Boards and Social Science Research." 2000. *American Association of University Professors.* 9 June 2005 <http://www.aaup.org/statements/Redbook/repirb.htm>.

Quayson, Ato. *Postcolonialism: Theory, Practice, or Process?* Cambridge, UK: Polity, 2000.

Rabillard, Sheila. "Absorption, Elimination, and the Hybrid: Some Impure Questions of Gender and Culture in the Trickster Drama of Tomson Highway." *Essays in Theatre* 12.1 (1993): 3–27.

Red Shirt, Delphine. *Bead on an Anthill: A Lakota Childhood.* Lincoln: U of Nebraska P, 1998.

———. *Turtle Lung Woman's Granddaughter.* Lincoln: U Nebraska P, 2002.

Redskins, Tricksters, and Puppy Stew. Dir. Drew Hayden Taylor. National Film Board of Canada, 2000.

Rice, Julian. *Before the Great Spirit: The Many Faces of Sioux Spirituality.* Albuquerque: U of New Mexico P, 1998.

———. "A Ventriloquy of Anthros: Densmore, Dorsey, Lame Deer, and Erdoes." *American Indian Quarterly* 18.2 (1994): 169–96.

Riggs, Stephan R. *Dakota Grammar, Texts, and Ethnography.* 1893.

Robertson, Paul. *The Power of the Land: Identity, Ethnicity, and Class among the Oglala Lakota.* New York: Routledge, 2002.

Robinson, Harry. *Nature Power: In the Spirit of an Okanagan Storyteller.* Vancouver BC: Douglas and McIntyre, 1992.

———. *Write It on Your Heart: The Epic World of an Okanagan Storyteller.* Penticton BC: Theytus, 1989.

Rose, LaVera. "Iyeska Win: Intermarriage and Ethnicity among the Lakota in the Nineteenth and Twentieth Centuries." MA thesis, Northern Arizona University, 1994.

Sahlins, Marshall. "Goodbye to *Tristes Tropes*: Ethnography in the Context of Modern World History." *Journal of Modern History* 65 (1993): 1–25.

Said, Edward. *Culture and Imperialism.* New York: Knopf, 1993.

Schweitzer, Marjorie M., ed. *American Indian Grandmothers: Traditions and Transitions.* Albuquerque: U of New Mexico P, 1999.

Silko, Leslie Marmon. *Ceremony.* New York: Penguin, 1977.

———. *Conversations with Leslie Marmon Silko.* Ed. Ellen L. Arnold. Jackson: UP of Mississippi, 2000.

Silvera, Makeda, ed. *The Other Woman: Women of Color in Contemporary Canadian Literature.* Toronto: Sister Vision, 1995.

Smith, Dorothy E. *Writing the Social: Critique, Theory, and Investigations.* Toronto ON: U of Toronto P, 1999.

Sneve, Virginia Driving Hawk. *Completing the Circle.* Lincoln: U of Nebraska P, 1995.

Spielmann, Roger. *"You're So Fat!" Exploring Ojibwe Discourse.* Toronto ON: U of Toronto P, 1998.

Spivak, Gayatri Chakravorty. "Can the Subaltern Speak?" *The Post-Colonial Studies Reader.* Ed. Bill Ashcroft, Gareth Griffiths, and Helen Tiffin. London: Routledge, 1995. 24–48.

———. "Foreword: Upon Reading the Companion to Postcolonial Studies." *A Companion to Postcolonial Studies.* Ed. Henry Schwarz and Ray Sangeeta. Malden: Blackwell, 2000. xv–xxii.

Spivak, Gayatri Chakravorty, Camille Paglia, Donna Landry, and Jane Gallop. "American Gender Studies Today." *Women: A Cultural Review* 10.2 (1999): 213–19.

Steinmetz, Paul B. *Pipe, Bible, and Peyote among the Oglala Lakota: A Study in Religious Identity.* Knoxville: U of Tennessee P, 1990.

Stevenson, Winona. "Indigenous Peoples' Oral Histories Raise Ethical Issues." *Oral History Association Newsletter* 33.2 (1999): 7.

Stewart, Omer C. *Peyote Religion: A History.* Norman: U of Oklahoma P, 1987.

WORKS CITED

Tedlock, Dennis. *The Spoken Word and the Work of Interpretation*. Philadelphia: U of Pennsylvania P, 1983.

Toelken, Barre. *The Dynamics of Folklore*. Boston: Houghton Mifflin, 1987.

Townsend, Robert B., and Meriam Belli. "Oral Historians and IRBs: Caution Urged as Rule Interpretations Vary." *Oral History Association Newsletter* 39.1 (2005): 1, 4–5.

"Tri-Council Policy Statement: Ethical Conduct for Research Involving Humans, 1998 (with 2000, 2002 updates)." *Interagency Advisory Panel on Research Ethics*. 2004. 9 June 2005 <http://www.pre.ethics.gc.ca/english/policystatement/policystatement.cfm>.

Tuhiwai Smith, Linda. *Decolonizing Methodologies: Research and Indigenous Peoples*. London: Zed, 1999.

United States Census Bureau. Census 2000. 2001. 9 June 2005 <http://factfinder.census.gov/servlet/BasicFactsServlet>.

"An Update: Excluding Oral History from IRB Review." *Oral History Association Newsletter* 38.1 (2004): 1.

Vickers, Scott B. *Native American Identities: From Stereotype to Archetype in Art and Literature*. Albuquerque: U of New Mexico P, 1998.

Wagoner, Paula L. *"They Treated Us Just Like Indians": The Worlds of Bennett County, South Dakota*. Lincoln: U of Nebraska P, 2002.

Walker, James R. *Lakota Belief and Ritual*. Ed. Raymond J. DeMallie and Elaine A. Jahner. 1896–1909. Lincoln: U of Nebraska P, 1980.

———. *Lakota Myth*. Ed. Elaine A. Jahner. 1896–1909. Lincoln: U of Nebraska P, 1983.

———. *Lakota Society*. Ed. Raymond J. DeMallie. 1896–1909. Lincoln: U of Nebraska P, 1982.

Weaver, Jace. *That the People Might Live: Native American Literatures and Native American Community*. New York: Oxford UP, 1997.

Whiteley, Peter M. *Rethinking Hopi Ethnography*. Washington DC: Smithsonian Institution P, 1998.

Wilson, Angela Cavender. "American Indian History or Non-Indian Perceptions of American Indian History?" *American Indian Quarterly* 20.1 (1996): 7–13.

Wise, Christopher, and R. Todd Wise. "A Conversation with Mary Brave Bird." *American Indian Quarterly* 24.3 (2000): 482–93.

Wissler, Clark. "Societies and Ceremonial Associations in the Oglala Division of the Teton-Dakota." *Anthropological Papers of the American Museum of Natural History* 11 (1912): 1–99.

Young Bear, Severt, and R. D. Theisz. *Standing in the Light: A Lakota Way of Seeing*. Lincoln: U of Nebraska P, 1994.

INDEX

vision quest (*hambleceya*), 10, 68, 111

wakan, 10, 110, 128

Wakan Tanka, 10, 77, 110, 111, 117, 122. See also *Tunkashila*

wasa (red paint), 15, 92

wasicu (white people), 92, 95, 107–8, 147n4. *See also* tradition, and colonization

wasna, 58, 61, 69, 92, 114

Waters, Emma, 132

Wheeler, Howard Act (Indian Reorganization Act), 35

White Buffalo Calf Woman, 26, 145n4

White Star, *72g*

wojapi, 58, 69, 114

Wounded Knee, xii, 26, 91, 108, 130, 140n8, 146n2, 147nn5–6

Young Bear, Severt, 66–67, 111

yuwipi ceremony, 10, 25, 69, 95, 141n5, 144nn2–3. *See also* dogs